WILLIAMS-SONOMA

Everyday Roasting

GENERAL EDITOR

Chuck Williams

RECIPES

Janeen Sarlin

PHOTOGRAPHY

Richard Eskite

TIME
LIFE
BOOKS

TIME-LIFE BOOKS

Time-Life Books is a division of Time Life Inc.
Time-Life is a trademark of Time Warner Inc. U.S.A.

TIME-LIFE CUSTOM PUBLISHING

Vice President and Publisher: Terry Newell
Managing Editor: Donia Ann Steele
Director of Acquisitions: Jennifer L. Pearce
Vice President of Sales and Marketing: Neil Levin
Director of Financial Operations: J. Brian Birky

WILLIAMS-SONOMA

Founder and Vice-Chairman: Chuck Williams
Book Buyer: Victoria Kalish

WELDON OWEN INC.

President: John Owen
Vice President and Publisher: Wendely Harvey
Chief Operating Officer: Larry Partington
Vice President International Sales: Stuart Laurence
Associate Publisher: Lisa Atwood
Senior Editor: Hannah Rahill
Consulting Editor: Norman Kolpas
Copy Editor: Sharon Silva
Design: Kari Perin, Perin+Perin
Production Director: Stephanie Sherman
Production Manager: Jen Dalton
Production Editor: Sarah Lemas
Food Stylist: George Dolese
Prop Stylist: Sara Slavin
Photo Production Coordinator: Juliann Harvey
Photo Assistant: Kevin Hossler
Food Styling Assistant: Jill Sorenson
Glossary Illustrations: Alice Harth

A NOTE ON WEIGHTS AND MEASURES

All recipes include customary U.S. and metric
measurements. Metric conversions are based on a
standard developed for these books and have been
rounded off. Actual weights may vary.

The Williams-Sonoma Lifestyles Series
conceived and produced by Weldon Owen Inc.
814 Montgomery Street, San Francisco, CA 94133

In collaboration with Williams-Sonoma
3250 Van Ness Avenue, San Francisco, CA 94109

Separations by Colourscan Overseas Co. Pte. Ltd.
Printed in Singapore by Tien Wah Press (Pte.) Ltd.

A WELDON OWEN PRODUCTION

Copyright © 1998 Weldon Owen Inc.
All rights reserved, including the right of repro-
duction in whole or in part in any form.

First printed in 1998
10 9 8 7 6 5 4 3 2 1

Library of Congress
Cataloging-in-Publication Data

Sarlin, Janeen.
    Everyday roasting / general editor, Chuck Williams;
  recipes, Janeen Sarlin; photography, Richard Eskite.
      p. cm. — (Williams-Sonoma lifestyles)
    Includes index.
    ISBN 0-7835-4616-5
    1. Roasting (Cookery) I. Williams, Chuck.
  II. Title. III. Series.
  TX690.S27 1998
  641.7′1— dc21   98-9458
                                        CIP

A NOTE ON NUTRITIONAL ANALYSIS

Each recipe is analyzed for significant nutrients per
serving. Not included in the analysis are ingredients
that are optional or added to taste, or are suggested
as an alternative or substitution either in the recipe
or in the recipe introduction or accompanying tip.
In recipes that yield a range of servings, the analysis
is for the middle of that range.

Contents

Welcome

Too many people associate roasting only with the holidays. That means they are missing out on some wonderful meals—meals that can make every day feel special.

Roasting is easy, and the results are unlike those from any other cooking method: rich brown crusts with juicy, flavorful interiors. You can roast nearly anything—not just meats, poultry, and seafood but also vegetables and fruits. In addition, everything tastes delicious for the time spent in the oven, despite the need for minimal preparation in many cases. If you want, you can easily roast every course of an evening meal, even on a busy weekday.

In a nutshell, that is why we've called this book *Everyday Roasting.* You'll find here 26 recipes for main-course roasts along with roasted appetizers, side dishes, and desserts.

Let me add a few words of advice, however. First, get to know your oven, calibrating it with a thermometer so you can set cooking temperatures accurately. And whatever you roast, always start with the best-quality, freshest ingredients you can find. The delectable meals you turn out will merit the extra effort. And who knows? Encouraged by a few successes, you may soon find yourself roasting every day!

Chuck Williams

The Pleasures of Roasting

From first course to last and everything in between, roasting delivers tasty food to the table with remarkable ease. Chicken with Garden Vegetables (at right; recipe on page 70) combines main course and side dish in a single pan. For dessert, Herb-Glazed Stuffed Figs (above; recipe on page 105) develop a delicious caramel glaze during the few minutes they spend in the oven.

Planning Meals Around the Oven

There's something wonderfully elemental about roasting, a tradition with roots that reach back to when the first foods were cooked over an open fire. Even though most roasting today is done in home ovens, the results retain a down-to-earth appeal: foods crusty and golden brown on the outside, juicy and flavorful inside, and with irresistible aromas that entice everyone within their reach.

Too many people, however, let the general fuss of the holidays convince them that roasting itself is complicated. Not so.

Consider that preparations are usually minimal: simple trussing, trimming, seasoning, stuffing, or marinating. Once the food is in the oven, your work is done—apart from occasional basting or glazing.

Consider, too, that many roasts cook in less than an hour, making it possible to put dinner on the table relatively quickly, even on the busiest weekday. As many of the recipes in this book demonstrate, you can also roast accompaniments in the same pan as the main course—and even pop an appetizer and dessert in the oven as well.

Preparing to Roast

TRUSSING POULTRY

Trussing keeps whole poultry compact for even cooking and more attractive results. Tuck the wing tips under the breast to keep them in place. Cross the drumsticks and tie their bony ends securely together with kitchen string.

TYING A FILLET

Whole fillets of beef (shown here), pork, or lamb roast more evenly when tied into compact, uniform shapes. Fold over the fillet's thin, tail-like end, and secure it with kitchen string. Continue tying string at 2–3-inch (5–7.5-cm) intervals.

TRIMMING AND SCORING CHOPS

Excess fat burns in the oven and membranes shrink, yielding misshapen results. When preparing chops, trim off excess fat with a paring knife. Slit the membranes all along the edges, making shallow vertical cuts at 1-inch (2.5-cm) intervals.

SAFETY TIPS

In recent years, widespread concerns about bacterial contamination of meats and poultry have made it necessary to be particularly vigilant when preparing these foods.

Before cooking large roasts, especially whole poultry, rinse thoroughly—including body cavities—with cold running water. Use clean implements and cutting boards for food preparation; after use, wash thoroughly with hot soapy water. Also wash your hands thoroughly with soap and hot running water before and after handling foods.

Leftover marinades are another common source of contamination. When basting with one, stop using it at least 10 minutes before the food is done, to ensure it reaches a heat level sufficient to kill any bacteria.

The Art of Roasting

Mastering Basic Skills

You can call roasting an art, but that doesn't mean you need any special talents to produce a masterpiece. Learning just a few basic steps will enable you to add your own touches of creativity.

Before you begin, have a general idea of how the method works. Roasting is the cooking of food in the dry, high-temperature heat of an oven. It is best suited to tender cuts of meat, to poultry, and to seafood. You can roast both large and small items.

A beautiful brown crust is one of the most appealing qualities of roasted foods. Contact with heat causes sugars and proteins to form compounds on the surface similar to caramel, thus the crust. Meanwhile, the heat slowly penetrates to the center, which stays juicy and flavorful.

Roasting usually proceeds most efficiently if you start with food at close to room temperature. That way the outside won't overcook before the center is done. For this same reason, the oven is preheated. Cooking temperatures vary with ingredients and size. In certain cases, the oven temperature is reduced at some point for more even cooking.

Adding Flavor and Moisture

The photographs at right demonstrate some of the most common ways to add artistry to roasting. All are concerned with enhancing flavor and conserving moisture.

Marinating is the most common way to flavor a roast. Wet marinades also add moisture, and they can have a tenderizing effect when they include an acidic liquid. Seasoning blends, known as dry marinades, are rubbed directly onto the surface of a roast. Stuffings, even simple ones tucked under poultry skin, also add savor while holding in moisture.

One of the most important tasks a cook can perform is to baste regularly. By spooning or brushing on pan juices, a marinade, or a glaze, the formation of a crust is promoted and the flesh stays moister. Tying bacon or pork fat on top of a roast, or stuffing butter or oil beneath poultry skin, also helps the flesh to baste itself as it cooks.

ROASTING OYSTERS IN SALT

The main purpose of roasting oysters on a bed of sea salt is to steady the irregularly shaped shells and yield an attractive presentation. But the salt also subtly seasons the creamy sauce that coats and moistens the bivalves.

MARINATING

Heavy-duty lock-top plastic bags make convenient marinating containers. Put the ingredients—here, a tomato-juice mixture for steak—in the bag. Press out the air, seal, and refrigerate.

STUFFING

You don't need to use whole poultry to benefit from stuffing. Here, flavorful ingredients are placed between the meat and skin to make Chicken with Sage and Prosciutto (recipe on page 40).

Many different kinds of vessels may be used for roasting, including copper, stainless-steel, or aluminum roasting pans; porcelain, enamel, or glass oven-to-table ware; and even jelly-roll (Swiss-roll) pans, rimmed baking sheets, and pie dishes. Choose a vessel that holds the ingredients comfortably, leaving room to spoon up or siphon juices for basting and allowing the oven's heat to circulate, without trapping moisture.

BROWNING

Larger roasts form their protective, flavorful crusts over time in the oven. Smaller, quicker-cooking cuts, such as these veal chops, benefit from quick browning in a frying pan to form a crust before roasting.

GLAZING

While basting keeps a roast moist and helps caramelize its surface, basting with a sweet glaze promotes an even more attractive and flavorful crust. A basting brush aids in applying a glaze.

Testing for Doneness

Looking for Sensory Cues

Down through the ages, cooks have developed a range of tests to show, with a glance, or a poke of a fork or knife, when a dish is done.

Whenever you roast, pay attention first to the suggested cooking time. Start testing for doneness at the earliest time suggested, using as your guide any sensory clues given in the recipe.

With smaller items, a close look may give some idea of doneness. For example, Roasted Oysters (recipe on page 24) firm up, whereas shrimp will curl and turn pink.

Whole roast poultry is traditionally tested by piercing the thigh (below, left) to see if its juices run clear. The flaky flesh of fish is easily separated with a knife tip (below, right), to see if it is cooked through. Vegetables or fruits are also easily tested with a sharp knife tip, which should meet no resistance once it has pierced the skin/surface.

Large cuts of meat are more problematic. Some chefs simply press a fingertip against a roast and assess its degree of doneness by the resistance they feel. An instant-read thermometer (see text, opposite), however, is a surer and safer proposition.

FLAKING SEAFOOD

Roast fish is done when its flesh firms up and loses its translucency, turning flaky and opaque. Gently run a knife tip across the flesh, checking between the flakes down into the center of the piece of fish.

CHECKING POULTRY JUICES

Whole poultry is done when the dark meat is cooked through and therefore no longer pink inside. To test for this, simply insert a knife tip, carving fork, or thin skewer into the thigh's thickest part: juices should run out clear, with no trace of pink or red.

BEEF

120°F (49°C) for rare

125°–130°F (52°–54°C)
for medium-rare

POULTRY

165°–170°F (74°–77°C) for chicken

162°–165°F (72°–74°C) for turkey breast

180°F (82°C) for turkey thigh

PORK

155°–160°F (68°–71°C)

LAMB

125°F (52°C) for rosy-rare

130°F (54°C) for medium-rare

140°F (60°C) for medium

Temperatures

The chart on the left offers internal temperature ranges for common degrees of doneness to which roasts are cooked. Note that after a roast has been removed from the oven, its interior temperature will continue to rise by 5°–10°F/2°–4°C beyond that given here.

The best way to judge a roast's internal temperature is with an instant-read thermometer, a utensil widely available today in cookware stores. At the earliest possible time the roast might be done, insert the thermometer into the thickest part of the roast, making sure that it does not touch bone. For poultry, the thermometer should be inserted into the thickest part of the thigh. Within a few seconds, the thermometer will register the temperature. If further roasting is required, remove the thermometer and check again in 5–15 minutes; the timing will depend on how much higher its internal temperature has to rise.

Serving Roast Foods

Preparing to Serve

Before carving, a large roast benefits from resting for 5–15 minutes after it leaves the oven, allowing its juices to settle back into the meat. Use a carving set, consisting of a two-pronged fork and a sharp knife with a flexible blade, and follow the instructions given below.

CARVING A BEEF FILLET

For the tenderest, juiciest results, always carve meat across the grain—perpendicular, not parallel, to its fibers. Here, a carving fork steadies a roast beef fillet being cut crosswise into thick slices with a large, sharp knife.

CARVING A CHICKEN

1. To carve a roast chicken, begin by moving the leg to locate the hip joint. Cut through the joint to remove the dark meat.

2. The breasts of small birds may be cut away from the rib cage whole for serving. For larger birds, carve the meat away in thin slices.

CARVING A LEG OF LAMB

Grasp the bone of a roast leg of lamb with a kitchen towel and hold at a 45-degree angle. Slice parallel to the bone, across the grain.

Presenting a Roast Meal

Beautifully browned and aromatic, any roast makes an impressive presentation. A little advance preparation, however, can make the meal even more memorable.

First, think about including a side dish in the roasting pan with the main course. Chunks of root vegetables, sliced onions, apples, and summer vegetables like eggplants (aubergines) are just a few of the options. Many of the recipes in this book feature such accompaniments, and you can easily adapt them to other roast dishes.

Presenting Roasts with Style

Cookware stores offer a number of practical, attractive options for presenting roasts. Each can add immeasurably to the ease and style with which you serve a meal.

For large, whole roasts, it makes good sense to use a wooden carving board (see Glossary, page 108). They not only look handsome, but also help steady the roast while you carve.

Large platters also show off roasts attractively. Be sure to choose one that suits the size, shape, and style of the food you are serving. It should allow room to do any carving, cutting, or other action comfortably.

Some roasts include sauces or gravies, which are most easily served from a sauce- or gravy boat with a ladle. You can also use a small serving bowl. Thinner sauces and gravies may be poured from small pitchers.

Many roasted dishes require no special serving techniques or presentations. In the case of the Apple-Roasted Pork Chops with Roast Applesauce shown here (recipe on page 35), the meat and its accompanying apple and onion slices are ready to serve from an oven-to-table ware roasting dish that looks elegant in its own right.

Planning Menus

The recipes in this book can be mixed and matched to create a wide variety of menus for every occasion. The ten menus provided here offer only a handful of the many combinations you can compose from the following pages. When planning any menu, choose courses with ingredients, seasonings, textures, and colors that complement one another. Add other components, as you wish, such as green salads, vegetable accompaniments, fresh-baked breads, and beverages.

Springtime Dinner

Roast Asparagus Salad
with Chèvre
PAGE 28

Veal Stuffed with
Spring Greens
PAGE 60

Pepper-and-Vanilla–Glazed
Pineapple with Yogurt Cheese
PAGE 98

Weeknight Celebration

Fast Mustard Lamb Chops
PAGE 31

Yam French Fries
PAGE 83

Lavender Glazed
Apple Tart
PAGE 106

Winter Repast

Butternut Squash Soup
PAGE 23

Cornish Hens au Poivre
PAGE 62

Honey-Pecan
Roast Pears
PAGE 102

Garden Supper

Tomato and Vegetable Soup
with Croutons
PAGE 20

Chicken with Garden Vegetables
PAGE 70

Black Plums en Croûte
PAGE 97

Summer Seafood Lunch

Warm Shrimp and
Haricots Verts Salad
PAGE 19

Roast Red Snapper with
Corn and Mushrooms
PAGE 39

Pepper-and-Vanilla–Glazed
Pineapple with Yogurt Cheese
PAGE 98

Southwestern Dinner

Corn and Roast
Poblano Soup
PAGE 27

Smoky and Spicy
Chicken Breasts
PAGE 80

Herb-Glazed Stuffed Figs
PAGE 105

Hearty Feast

Mint-and-Chive–Marinated
Leg of Lamb
PAGE 51

Niçoise Mushrooms
PAGE 85

Lavender Glazed
Apple Tart
PAGE 106

Vegetarian Harvest

Baby Artichokes with
Sunflower Seeds
PAGE 94

Summer Vegetables
and Caponata with Polenta
PAGE 43

Roast Bananas with Cinnamon
Ice Cream and Chocolate Sauce
PAGE 101

Late-Summer Supper

Oven-Baked Brown Rice
with Roast Tomatoes
PAGE 86

Saffron-Scented Halibut
with Spinach, Zucchini,
and Tomato
PAGE 66

Black Plums en Croûte
PAGE 97

Happy Holidays

Roasted Oysters
PAGE 24

Tarragon Beef Fillet with
Madeira and Mushroom Sauce
PAGE 36

Honey-Pecan
Roast Pears
PAGE 102

Warm Shrimp and Haricots Verts Salad

PREP TIME: 10 MINUTES,
PLUS 30 MINUTES FOR
MARINATING

COOKING TIME: 15 MINUTES

INGREDIENTS

1½ lb (750 g) shrimp (prawns),
    peeled and deveined

2 large cloves garlic, minced

1 teaspoon dried thyme

½ teaspoon red pepper flakes

juice of 2 lemons

about 6 tablespoons (3 fl oz/90 ml)
    olive oil

2½ lb (1.25 kg) haricots verts or
    young, tender green beans

coarse salt for roasting, plus extra
    to taste

8–12 oil-packed sun-dried tomatoes,
    drained and slivered

⅓ cup (½ oz/15 g) chopped fresh
    flat-leaf (Italian) parsley

ground pepper to taste

8 large red-leaf lettuce leaves

1 small bunch fresh chives, snipped

PREP TIP: You can cook the haricots verts up to 1 day in advance. Undercook them slightly, drain, trim, and refrigerate. Just before serving, reheat the beans in the hot dressing in the frying pan, tossing and stirring for about 3 minutes. Arrange on the lettuce and serve immediately.

The pink, spicy roasted shrimp atop the dark green beans make a spectacular presentation on individual plates for a sit-down dinner. Or mound them on a large platter for a beautiful buffet dish to serve alongside a roasted fillet of beef (page 36).

SERVES 8

✹ In a nonaluminum dish, combine the shrimp, garlic, thyme, red pepper flakes, half of the lemon juice, and 4 tablespoons (2 fl oz/60 ml) of the olive oil. Toss well. Cover and refrigerate for at least 30 minutes or for up to 1 hour.

✹ Meanwhile, bring a large saucepan three-fourths full of salted water to a boil. Add the beans and boil until barely tender, about 2 minutes. Drain and immediately plunge into very cold water to stop the cooking. Drain again and trim off the stem ends; leave the tiny tips of the beans intact. Set aside.

✹ Preheat an oven to 450°F (230°C).

✹ Sprinkle a rimmed baking sheet with coarse salt. Remove the shrimp from the marinade, reserving the marinade, and arrange in a single layer on the prepared pan. Roast until they turn pink, begin to curl, and are tender, 7–8 minutes.

✹ Meanwhile, in a large frying pan over high heat, bring the marinade to a boil. Cook for 3–4 minutes. Stir in the sun-dried tomatoes and the parsley. Add the remaining 2 tablespoons olive oil and as much of the remaining lemon juice as needed to create enough dressing for the salad, about ½ cup (4 fl oz/125 ml) total. Season with salt and pepper. Spoon 2–3 tablespoons of the warm dressing over the beans to reheat and toss to coat.

✹ Line individual salad plates with the lettuce leaves. Divide the warm beans evenly among the plates, mounding them in the center. Arrange the shrimp on the beans, again dividing evenly, and drizzle about 1 tablespoon warm dressing over each salad. Garnish with the chives and serve immediately.

NUTRITIONAL ANALYSIS PER SERVING: Calories 236 (Kilojoules 991); Protein 18 g; Carbohydrates 15 g; Total Fat 13 g; Saturated Fat 2 g; Cholesterol 105 mg; Sodium 151 mg; Dietary Fiber 4 g

Tomato and Garden Vegetable Soup with Croutons

SERVES 10–12

PREP TIME: 25 MINUTES

COOKING TIME: 45 MINUTES

INGREDIENTS

6–8 large firm, ripe tomatoes, halved crosswise

about 1½ cups (12 fl oz/375 ml) tomato juice, or as needed

1 head garlic

2 each zucchini (courgettes) and yellow summer squashes, diced

4 carrots, peeled and diced

4 celery stalks, finely diced

4 potatoes, peeled and diced

kernels cut from 4 ears of corn

2 yellow onions, chopped

2 leeks, white part only, chopped

coarse salt and ground pepper to taste

1 baguette, cut into small cubes

2 teaspoons unsalted butter

3 tablespoons olive oil, plus more as needed

2 tablespoons chopped fresh flat-leaf (Italian) parsley, plus minced parsley for garnish

1 tablespoon chopped fresh basil, plus minced basil for garnish

1 tablespoon chopped fresh summer savory, plus minced summer savory for garnish

8 cups (64 fl oz/2 l) chicken broth

7 or 8 parsley sprigs, tied together

½ cup (2 oz/60 g) grated Parmesan cheese, plus extra for garnish

❁ Preheat an oven to 425°F (220°C). Line 2 rimmed baking sheets with aluminum foil and brush with olive oil.

❁ Working over a sieve placed over a large measuring pitcher, gently squeeze out the seeds from the tomatoes, capturing all the juices. Press the contents through the sieve. Add enough tomato juice to measure 3 cups (24 fl oz/750 ml) total. Set aside. Coarsely chop the tomato halves. Separate the garlic head into cloves, leaving the skins intact, and reserve 3 cloves. In batches, arrange the tomatoes, the remaining unpeeled garlic cloves, the zucchini, yellow squashes, carrots, celery, potatoes, corn, and 1 each of the chopped onions and leeks on the prepared baking sheets. Season each batch with a pinch of salt and a few drops of olive oil. Roast until lightly browned on the edges and nearly tender, 10–15 minutes. Remove from the oven. When the garlic has cooled slightly, gently squeeze the cloves free of their skins, leaving the soft cloves whole. Then arrange the bread cubes on a baking sheet and toast until lightly browned, about 7 minutes. Set aside.

❁ Meanwhile, peel and mince 2 of the reserved garlic cloves. In a large stockpot over medium heat, melt the butter and 1 tablespoon of the olive oil, add the minced garlic and the remaining chopped onion and leek, and sauté until soft, 5–6 minutes. Add all of the roasted vegetables, the tomato juice, and the chopped parsley, basil, and savory. Cook, stirring frequently, until the vegetables are coated with the butter and oil. Season with salt and pepper, and add the broth and parsley stems. Bring to a boil, reduce the heat to low, cover partially, and simmer until tender, about 15 minutes. Discard the parsley stems. Adjust the seasonings.

❁ While the soup simmers, in a large sauté pan over medium-high heat, warm the remaining 2 tablespoons oil. Halve the remaining garlic clove, and sauté until lightly browned, about 4 minutes. Discard the garlic. Working in batches, sauté the bread cubes, tossing constantly, until browned and crisp, about 5 minutes. Transfer to paper towels to drain, then sprinkle with the ½ cup (2 oz/60 g) Parmesan.

❁ To serve, ladle into warmed soup bowls, top with the croutons, and sprinkle with the minced herbs and grated Parmesan. Serve at once.

NUTRITIONAL ANALYSIS PER SERVING: Calories 374 (Kilojoules 1,571); Protein 13 g; Carbohydrates 61 g; Total Fat 10 g; Saturated Fat 2 g; Cholesterol 6 mg; Sodium 1,249 mg; Dietary Fiber 8 g

Butternut Squash Soup

PREP TIME: 30 MINUTES

COOKING TIME: 1¼ HOURS

INGREDIENTS

1 butternut squash, 3½–4 lb
(1.75–2 kg), halved, seeds and
fibers discarded, peeled, and
flesh cubed

4 leeks

1 large yellow onion, chopped

coarse salt and ground black pepper
to taste

2 tablespoons olive oil

3 carrots

5–6 cups (40–48 fl oz/1.25–1.5 l)
chicken broth

1 teaspoon unsalted butter

1 celery stalk with leaves, chopped

1 teaspoon minced fresh thyme

pinch of cayenne pepper

pinch of freshly grated nutmeg, plus
extra to taste

COOKING TIP: You can substitute
other winter squash varieties such as
Hubbard or acorn for the butternut
squash.

At the first sign of hard-skinned squash and colorful fall leaves,
serve this creamy, golden soup as a starter.

SERVES 6

❋ Preheat an oven to 425°F (220°C). Line 2 or 3 rimmed baking sheets
with aluminum foil and brush with oil. Arrange the squash in a single
layer on the prepared pans. Roast until browned on the edges, 13–15 minutes. Meanwhile, chop 2 of the leeks, including about 1 inch (2.5 cm) of
the green. Remove the squash from the oven and set aside. Using the
same pans, arrange the chopped leeks and onion in a single layer, and
roast until browned on the edges, 10–12 minutes.

❋ While the chopped leeks and onion are roasting, julienne the remaining 2 leeks, using the white parts only. Using the same pans, scatter the
julienned leeks in a single layer, season with salt and pepper, and drizzle with 1 tablespoon of the olive oil. Roast until crisp and browned,
12–13 minutes. Transfer to a paper towel–lined plate and set aside.

❋ Peel and julienne 2 of the carrots. In a small frying pan over low heat,
combine 2 tablespoons of the chicken broth and the julienned carrots.
Cover partially and "sweat" the carrots until barely tender and the broth
has evaporated, about 5 minutes. Transfer to the plate with the leeks.

❋ Meanwhile, peel and chop the remaining carrot. In a stockpot over
medium heat, melt the butter with the remaining 1 tablespoon oil. Add
the celery and chopped carrot and sauté until the vegetables begin to
soften, 5–6 minutes. Add the roasted chopped leeks, squash, and onion;
cook for 1–2 minutes. Add the thyme, cayenne, nutmeg, and season
with salt and pepper. Continue to cook, stirring, until the vegetables
glisten, about 2 minutes. Add enough of the remaining chicken broth to
cover the vegetables in the pot by ½ inch (12 mm). Cover and bring to a
boil. Reduce the heat to low, position the lid ajar, and simmer until all
the vegetables are soft, about 20 minutes. Let cool for a few minutes,
then, working in batches, purée the soup in a food processor.

❋ Return the soup to the stockpot, taste and adjust the seasonings, and
reheat gently. Whisk in a few nutmeg gratings, ladle into warmed soup
bowls, and garnish with the reserved carrots and leeks.

NUTRITIONAL ANALYSIS PER SERVING: Calories 257 (Kilojoules 1,079); Protein 6 g;
Carbohydrates 46 g; Total Fat 8 g; Saturated Fat 1; Cholesterol 2 mg; Sodium 961 mg;
Dietary Fiber 7 g

Roasted Oysters

PREP TIME: 20 MINUTES

COOKING TIME: 5 MINUTES

INGREDIENTS

coarse salt for roasting, plus extra
to taste

6 green (spring) onions, including
about 2 inches of green, coarsely
chopped

1 small head radicchio, coarsely
chopped

½ bunch watercress, stems removed

½ bunch fresh flat-leaf (Italian)
parsley, stems removed

20 large fresh basil leaves, coarsely
chopped

2 lemons

2 tablespoons extra-virgin olive oil

1 tablespoon balsamic vinegar

½ cup (4 fl oz/125 ml) mayonnaise

ground pepper to taste

24 oysters on the half shell

¼ cup (1 oz/30 g) fine dried bread
crumbs

For a spectacular presentation, ask your fishmonger for some seaweed to create a serving bed for these succulent bivalves. The peppery, creamy green coating suggests ambrosia.

SERVES 6

❋ Preheat an oven to 500°F (260°C). Line a rimmed baking sheet with aluminum foil. Pour in enough salt to form a layer about ½ inch (12 mm) deep and set aside.

❋ In a food processor, combine the green onions, radicchio, watercress, parsley, and basil. Process until evenly chopped. Set aside. Grate the zest from 1 of the lemons into a bowl, then juice the lemon, adding the juice to the bowl. Add the olive oil and vinegar and whisk until blended. Whisk in the mayonnaise and season with coarse salt and pepper. Fold in the herb mixture to form a creamy topping.

❋ Using a thin-bladed knife, completely mask each oyster with about 1 tablespoon of the topping. Set the oysters snugly in the salt layer, allowing space around each one. Sprinkle about ¼ teaspoon of the bread crumbs on each oyster.

❋ Roast until the crumbs are lightly browned, 5–6 minutes.

❋ When the oysters are ready, divide them among the plates. Cut the remaining lemon into 6 wedges and garnish each serving with a wedge. Serve immediately.

NUTRITIONAL ANALYSIS PER SERVING: Calories 243 (Kilojoules 1,021); Protein 6 g; Carbohydrates 9 g; Total Fat 21 g; Saturated Fat 3 g; Cholesterol 42 mg; Sodium 217 mg; Dietary Fiber 1 g

Corn and Roast Poblano Soup

PREP TIME: 25 MINUTES

COOKING TIME: 45 MINUTES

INGREDIENTS

6 or 7 large poblano chiles

8 cups (64 fl oz/2 l) milk

2 tablespoons cumin seeds

1 or 2 chipotle chiles

2 bay leaves

1 large fresh rosemary sprig or
½ teaspoon dried rosemary

2 tablespoons unsalted butter

2 tablespoons olive oil

2 large yellow onions, diced

2 teaspoons salt

4–6 cloves garlic, minced

2 teaspoons ground cumin

kernels cut from 8 ears of corn
(about 8 cups/3 lb/1.5 kg)

6 green (spring) onions, including
about 2 inches (5 cm) of green,
finely chopped

Roasting the poblano chiles to give them a richer, mellower, sweeter taste is one of the secrets to making this robust soup. The other secret is to steep the cumin seeds, bay leaves, rosemary, and chipotle chiles in warm milk to infuse the milk with their flavors.

SERVES 6

✳ Preheat a broiler (griller). Place the poblano chiles on a baking sheet. Broil (grill), turning as needed, until the skins blacken and blister. Remove from the broiler, drape the chiles loosely with aluminum foil, and let cool for 10–15 minutes. Working under cold running water, peel away the skins. Slit lengthwise and remove the stems, seeds, and ribs. Pat the chiles dry and then dice them. Set aside.

✳ Pour the milk into a heavy saucepan. In a small, dry frying pan over high heat, toast the cumin seeds, shaking the pan constantly until they are aromatic and begin to change color, about 4 minutes. Remove from the heat and immediately add to the milk. Add the chipotle chiles, bay leaves, and rosemary and place over low heat. Cover and bring to a gentle simmer; do not allow to boil. Remove from the heat and let stand, covered, for 20 minutes.

✳ Meanwhile, in a stockpot over medium heat, melt the butter with the olive oil. Add the onions and salt and sauté, stirring, until the onions are soft and golden brown, 15–20 minutes. Reduce the heat to medium-low, add the garlic and ground cumin, and sauté, stirring constantly, until aromatic, about 5 minutes. Stir in the corn and poblano chiles, and continue cooking until the corn is lightly browned, about 5 minutes. Using a fine-mesh sieve, strain the milk into the corn mixture. Bring to a gentle simmer and continue to simmer until the flavors have melded, about 15 minutes. Remove from the heat and let cool for a few minutes.

✳ In a food processor, purée one-third of the soup. Return the purée to the stockpot, stirring well. If necessary, place over low heat to reheat gently. Taste and adjust the seasonings. Ladle into warmed soup bowls, garnish with the green onions, and serve.

NUTRITIONAL ANALYSIS PER SERVING: Calories 542 (Kilojoules 2,276); Protein 21 g; Carbohydrates 75 g; Total Fat 23 g; Saturated Fat 10 g; Cholesterol 56 mg; Sodium 985 mg; Dietary Fiber 10 g

Roast Asparagus Salad with Chèvre

PREP TIME: 15 MINUTES

COOKING TIME: 15 MINUTES

INGREDIENTS
1½ lb (750 g) asparagus

coarse salt and ground pepper
    to taste

about ½ teaspoon extra-virgin olive oil

FOR THE DRESSING
2 tablespoons lemon juice

2 tablespoons extra-virgin olive oil

2 tablespoons olive oil

1 tablespoon Dijon mustard

3–4 tablespoons snipped fresh chives

ground pepper to taste

6 green (spring) onions, including
    about 2 inches (5 cm) of green,
    chopped

7–8 cups (7–8 oz/220–250 g) mixed
    baby salad greens

2 cups (12 oz/375 g) cherry toma-
    toes, red or mixed red and yellow,
    stems removed

¼ lb (125 g) herbed chèvre, cut into
    6 slices

MAKE-AHEAD TIP: The dressing can
be made up to 2 weeks in advance and
stored, covered, in a nonaluminum
container in the refrigerator. Bring
to room temperature before using.

Pass hot, crust-seeded semolina or whole-grain bread at the
table for mopping up extra dressing from the plate.

SERVES 6

❊ Preheat an oven to 400°F (200°C). Line a rimmed baking sheet with
aluminum foil and brush with olive oil.

❊ Snap off any tough ends from the asparagus spears and trim the break
with a sharp knife. Using a vegetable peeler, and starting just below the
tip, peel the skin off each spear, down to the end. Arrange the spears in
a single layer on the prepared pan, season with salt and pepper, and
drizzle with the extra-virgin olive oil. Roast until tender, 12–14 minutes.
Transfer to a plate and set aside.

❊ To make the dressing, in a small bowl, whisk together the lemon
juice, extra-virgin olive oil, olive oil, and mustard. Stir in the chives, and
season with pepper.

❊ Spoon about 2 tablespoons of the dressing over the asparagus and let
stand while tossing the salad.

❊ In a large bowl, gently toss together the green onions and the salad
greens. Add the tomatoes. Drizzle just enough of the dressing onto the
salad for the greens to glisten, and toss again. (You may not need to use
all of the dressing.) Immediately mound the salad in the center of large
individual salad plates. Place a slice of chèvre on top of each mound of
greens, and arrange asparagus spears around the perimeter of each plate,
dividing them equally. Drizzle a few extra drops of the remaining dressing over the chèvre. Serve immediately.

NUTRITIONAL ANALYSIS PER SERVING: Calories 174 (Kilojoules 731); Protein 7 g;
Carbohydrates 8 g; Total Fat 14 g; Saturated Fat 4 g; Cholesterol 20 mg; Sodium 183 mg;
Dietary Fiber 2 g

Fast Mustard Lamb Chops

PREP TIME: 5 MINUTES,
    PLUS 10 MINUTES FOR
    MARINATING

COOKING TIME: 10 MINUTES

INGREDIENTS

8 baby loin lamb chops, each 4–5 oz (125–155 g) and 1–1¼ inches (2.5–3 cm) thick, trimmed of fat and edges scored

ground pepper to taste

4–5 tablespoons grainy Dijon mustard, or as needed

fresh flat-leaf (Italian) parsley sprigs

This recipe is for the person who loves good food but has little time to cook. The succulent, tender loin lamb chops roast in only 10 minutes. Serve with quick-cooking couscous laced with toasted pine nuts.

SERVES 4

❀ Preheat an oven to 500°F (260°C). Lightly oil a shallow roasting pan.

❀ Rub both sides of each chop with pepper and place in the prepared roasting pan. Slather about 1 teaspoon mustard on one side of each chop and bring to room temperature, 10–15 minutes.

❀ Roast, mustard side up, until the chops are browned on top, about 5 minutes. Turn the chops over and slather about 1 teaspoon mustard on the second side. Continue to roast until the meat is pink in the center when cut into with a knife, about 5 minutes longer or until done to your liking. The roasting time will depend upon the thickness of the chops and personal preference.

❀ Divide the chops among warmed individual plates, placing 2 chops on each plate. Garnish with parsley and serve immediately.

NUTRITIONAL ANALYSIS PER SERVING: Calories 251 (Kilojoules 1,054); Protein 29 g; Carbohydrates 0 g; Total Fat 12 g; Saturated Fat 4 g; Cholesterol 95 mg; Sodium 480 mg; Dietary Fiber 0 g

Spring Chicken with Saffron and Lemon

PREP TIME: 25 MINUTES,
PLUS 24 HOURS FOR
MARINATING

COOKING TIME: 1½ HOURS

INGREDIENTS

2 large pinches of saffron threads
(about 1 heaping teaspoon)

1 tablespoon coarse salt

½–¾ teaspoon coarsely ground
pepper

2 young chickens, 3 lb (1.5 kg) each

2 lemons, thinly sliced, plus 1 lemon,
cut into wedges

several fresh rosemary sprigs, plus
extra for garnish

⅔ cup (5 fl oz/160 ml) chicken broth

SERVING TIP: If you like, serve the
birds cold for a picnic or cut the cold
meat from the carcass for use in a
salad or sandwich for lunch.

The combination of fresh lemon and rosemary and aromatic
golden saffron is hard to beat. Season the chickens a day or more
before roasting to infuse the flesh with the seasonings.

SERVES 6

❊ In a mortar, grind together the saffron threads, salt, and pepper with
a pestle. Rinse the chickens and pat dry with paper towels. Carefully
slide your fingers under the skin on each chicken breast, separating it
from the breast and thigh but leaving it attached. Rub the saffron mixture on the meat under the skin, over the top of the skin, and inside
the cavities of both chickens. Place the lemon slices and a few sprigs of
rosemary here and there under the skin as well as inside the cavity of
each chicken. Place the chickens side by side in a large nonaluminum
bowl, cover tightly with plastic wrap, and refrigerate for at least 24 hours
or for up to 36 hours.

❊ Bring the chickens to room temperature before roasting, about 1 hour.
Preheat an oven to 400°F (200°C). Place the chickens, breast sides down,
on a rack in a large roasting pan. Tuck the wing tips underneath the breasts,
then cross the drumsticks and, using kitchen string, tie the legs together.

❊ Roast for 15 minutes. Turn breast sides up and continue to roast, basting every 10 minutes with the pan juices during the last 30 minutes,
until the skin is crisp and brown and the juices run clear when the thigh
is pierced at the thickest part with a fork, 1–1½ hours total. Alternatively,
insert an instant-read thermometer into the thickest part of the thigh
away from the bone; it should register 165°–170°F (74°–77°C). If the
chickens are browning too fast, reduce the oven temperature to 350°F
(180°C), and continue to roast until done. Transfer the chickens to a
cutting board and let rest for at least 15 minutes before carving.

❊ Meanwhile, place the pan over high heat. Add the broth and deglaze
the pan, stirring with a wooden spoon to remove any browned bits from
the pan bottom. Bring to a boil and boil until reduced by one-half, about
5 minutes. Spoon off the fat from the pan juices, then strain through a
fine-mesh sieve into a warmed sauceboat.

❊ Arrange the chicken on a warmed platter. Garnish with rosemary and
lemon wedges. Snip the strings and carve. Pass the pan juices.

NUTRITIONAL ANALYSIS PER SERVING: Calories 493 (Kilojoules 2,071); Protein 55 g;
Carbohydrates 6 g; Total Fat 28 g; Saturated Fat 8 g; Cholesterol 176 mg; Sodium 1,013 mg;
Dietary Fiber 0 g

Apple-Roasted Pork Chops with Roast Applesauce

PREP TIME: 40 MINUTES,
PLUS 4 HOURS FOR
MARINATING

COOKING TIME: 50 MINUTES

INGREDIENTS

6 loin pork chops, each 7–8 oz
(220–250 g) and 1 inch (2.5 cm)
thick, trimmed of fat and edges
scored

FOR THE MARINADE

⅔ cup (5 fl oz/160 ml) apple cider

1 teaspoon olive oil

1 small yellow onion, sliced

1 tablespoon fresh thyme leaves

2 cloves garlic, minced

1 teaspoon peppercorns

salt and ground pepper to taste

2 tart green apples

1 tablespoon unsalted butter

1 tablespoon olive oil, or as needed

1 generous cup (3 oz/90 g) dried
apples

1 yellow onion, sliced

¼ cup (2 fl oz/60 ml) apple cider

¼ cup (2 fl oz/60 ml) Calvados or
other dry apple brandy

FOR THE ROAST APPLESAUCE

8–10 tart apples, half green and half
red, quartered

¾ cup (6 fl oz/180 ml) water

pinch of salt

¼ cup (2 oz/60 g) sugar, or to taste

½ teaspoon ground cinnamon

Apple cider tenderizes the meat, while the thyme, garlic, and onion add flavor. Serve with fried potatoes.

SERVES 6

❋ Marinate the pork chops: Place the chops in a large, heavy-duty lock-top plastic bag or a large nonaluminum dish. Add the cider, olive oil, onion, thyme, garlic, and peppercorns to the bag or dish. Press out the air and seal the bag securely, or cover the dish with plastic wrap. Refrigerate for at least 4 hours or for up to 24 hours, turning occasionally.

❋ Preheat an oven to 400°F (200°C). Remove the chops from the marinade, pat dry with paper towels, and season with salt and pepper. Discard the marinade. Peel, core, and slice the fresh apples. In a large sauté pan over high heat, melt the butter with the olive oil. When the foam subsides, add the chops and sear, turning once, until browned, about 2 minutes on each side. Meanwhile, scatter the fresh and dried apples and onion slices in a baking dish large enough to hold the chops in a single layer. Set the browned chops on top of the apple and onion, pour the apple cider around the chops, and cover the dish.

❋ To make the applesauce, in a large baking dish with a lid, combine the apples, water, and salt. Place both baking dishes in the oven.

❋ Roast for 10 minutes, then reduce the temperature to 350°F (180°C) and cover the baking dish holding the applesauce. Continue to cook the chops until nearly tender, about 25 minutes longer. Uncover and baste with the Calvados. Continue to roast until the juices run clear and the chops are tender, about 10 minutes longer. At the same time, cook the apples, stirring occasionally, until soft, about 30 minutes longer.

❋ Remove from the oven. Working in batches, pass the roasted apple quarters through a food mill placed over a bowl; discard the skins and seeds. (Alternatively, purée in a food processor, then pass the purée through a sieve into a bowl. Press with a rubber spatula to push as much applesauce through as possible.) Sweeten the applesauce with the sugar. You should have about 4 cups (2¼ lb/1.1 kg). Transfer the sauce to a warmed bowl and sprinkle the cinnamon on top.

❋ Serve the pork chops directly from the dish. Pass the applesauce.

NUTRITIONAL ANALYSIS PER SERVING: Calories 533 (Kilojoules 2,239); Protein 33 g; Carbohydrates 67 g; Total Fat 14 g; Saturated Fat 5 g; Cholesterol 93 mg; Sodium 115 mg; Dietary Fiber 6 g

Tarragon Beef Fillet with Madeira and Mushroom Sauce

PREP TIME: 30 MINUTES,
PLUS 30 MINUTES FOR
MARINATING

COOKING TIME: 1 HOUR

INGREDIENTS

1 whole beef fillet, 3–3½ lb
(1.5–1.75 kg), trimmed of fat
and sinews

1 teaspoon dried tarragon

1 teaspoon ground pepper, or
to taste

about 2 tablespoons Madeira wine

FOR THE MUSHROOM SAUCE

6 dried shiitake mushrooms, soaked
in warm water to cover for
30 minutes

1 oz (30 g) dried porcini or morel
mushrooms, soaked in warm
water to cover for 30 minutes

about 2 tablespoons olive oil

8 fresh oyster mushrooms, brushed
clean and tough stems removed,
sliced

6 oz (185 g) fresh button mushrooms,
brushed clean and sliced

about ⅓ cup (3 fl oz/80 ml) Madeira
wine

salt and ground pepper to taste

2 tablespoons unsalted butter

4 shallots, chopped

1 tablespoon chopped fresh tarragon

1 cup (8 fl oz/250 ml) beef broth

fresh watercress sprigs

Wrapping the roasted beef fillet in parchment paper and news-paper to rest keeps the juices inside the meat.

SERVES 8–10

❋ Preheat an oven to 500°F (260°C). Lightly oil a rimmed baking sheet. Rub the beef fillet with the tarragon and pepper. Fold the thin tail of meat under to make an evenly thick roast. Tie the meat with kitchen string at regular intervals 2–3 inches (5–7.5 cm) apart. Place the meat on the prepared baking sheet. Drizzle the Madeira over the beef and let marinate at room temperature for 30 minutes before roasting.

❋ Place the fillet in the oven. Immediately reduce the heat to 450°F (230°C) and roast the meat for 25 minutes for rare, or 30 minutes for medium-rare. Meanwhile, prepare several thicknesses of newspaper and top with a sheet of parchment (baking) paper. When the beef is ready, transfer it to the parchment and roll it up in the paper, enclosing completely. Then roll the newspapers around it. Let rest for 20–25 minutes.

❋ Meanwhile, prepare the sauce: Squeeze the water from the rehydrated mushrooms. Remove and discard any tough stems and thinly slice the tops. In a large sauté pan over high heat, warm enough of the olive oil to form a film on the pan bottom. Working in batches, sauté each variety of dried and fresh mushroom separately, shaking the pan constantly, until they no longer give off any moisture, 4–5 minutes for each batch. Add a splash of Madeira to each batch and cook for about 1 minute longer. Season with salt and pepper. Transfer to a bowl.

❋ Return the sauté pan to medium heat and melt the butter. Add the shallots and a little oil if necessary to prevent scorching, and sauté until soft, about 7 minutes. Season with the tarragon and pepper. Add the remaining Madeira (there should be about 3 tablespoons) and bring to a boil. Cook for 3 minutes. Return the mushrooms and their juices to the pan, add the broth, and bring to a boil. Reduce the heat to low and simmer, uncovered, until the liquid is reduced by one-half, about 20 minutes. Adjust the seasonings. Transfer to a warmed sauceboat.

❋ To serve, unwrap the beef, snip the strings, and cut across the grain into slices. Arrange on a warmed platter, spoon on a bit of the sauce, and garnish with watercress. Pass the remaining sauce at the table.

NUTRITIONAL ANALYSIS PER SERVING: Calories 363 (Kilojoules 1,525); Protein 36 g; Carbohydrates 7 g; Total Fat 19 g; Saturated Fat 7 g; Cholesterol 109 mg; Sodium 191 mg; Dietary Fiber 2 g

Roast Red Snapper with Corn and Mushrooms

PREP TIME: 20 MINUTES

COOKING TIME: 25 MINUTES

INGREDIENTS

1 yellow onion, chopped

3 cups (18 oz/560 g) fresh corn
  kernels (from 3 ears of corn)

6 mushrooms, brushed clean and
  thinly sliced

3 tablespoons snipped fresh chives

10 large fresh basil leaves, finely
  shredded

pinch of ground coriander, plus
  ½ teaspoon

1½ teaspoons dried basil

coarse salt to taste, plus ½ teaspoon
  salt

ground pepper to taste, plus
  ½ teaspoon

3 tablespoons olive oil

2 tablespoons lime juice, plus 1 lime,
  thinly sliced

about ⅔ cup (2½ oz/75 g) rice flour

6 red snapper fillets with skin intact,
  about 6 oz (185 g) each

Rice flour forms a thin crust on the fillets that are first seared and then roasted on a bed of basil-seasoned vegetables. The characteristic snapper flavor marries well with the mild acidity of the lime juice. Pacific snapper or weakfish would also work nicely.

SERVES 6

❊ Preheat an oven to 450°F (230°C). Lightly oil 2 baking dishes large enough to hold the fish fillets in a single layer.

❊ In a bowl, stir together the onion, corn kernels, mushrooms, chives, and half of the fresh basil. Season with a pinch of ground coriander, ½ teaspoon of the dried basil, and salt and pepper. Mix well and add 2 tablespoons of the olive oil and the lime juice. Toss lightly. Divide the vegetables between the prepared baking dishes, and scatter the lime slices over the top.

❊ In another shallow bowl, stir together the rice flour, the remaining 1 teaspoon dried basil, and the ½ teaspoon each ground coriander, salt, and pepper. Rinse the fish fillets and pat dry with paper towels. Dredge the fillets in the seasoned flour, tapping off any excess.

❊ In a large nonstick frying pan over high heat, warm about 1 tablespoon of the olive oil. Add the fillets and sear, turning once, until lightly browned, about 2 minutes on each side. Transfer the fillets, skin sides up, to the baking dishes, placing them on top of the vegetables and leaving room around each fillet to ensure even cooking.

❊ Roast until the vegetables are tender and the fillets are opaque throughout when pierced with a knife, about 20 minutes.

❊ Remove from the oven and garnish with the remaining fresh basil. Serve immediately, directly from the baking dishes.

NUTRITIONAL ANALYSIS PER SERVING: Calories 422 (Kilojoules 1,772); Protein 39 g; Carbohydrates 31 g; Total Fat 16 g; Saturated Fat 2 g; Cholesterol 63 mg; Sodium 246 mg; Dietary Fiber 4 g

Chicken with Sage and Prosciutto

PREP TIME: 20 MINUTES

COOKING TIME: 55 MINUTES

INGREDIENTS

6 chicken breast halves, about 6 oz
(185 g) each

6 chicken drumsticks, about 4 oz
(125 g) each

6 chicken thighs, about 5 oz (155 g)
each

18 thin slices prosciutto

18 fresh sage leaves, plus sage sprigs
for garnish

1½–2 tablespoons olive oil

coarse salt and ground pepper
to taste

PREP TIP: For variation, substitute
1 thin yellow onion slice and 2 or 3
thin tart apple slices for each prosciutto slice and sage leaf.

Very little effort is needed to prepare this dish, and it is an easy recipe to double for a large crowd. The pleasant mustiness of the sage permeates the chicken hot from the oven. Any leftovers are delicious served cold the next day, when the distinctive flavor of the prosciutto predominates. Oven-Baked Brown Rice with Roast Tomatoes (page 86) works well as a side dish.

SERVES 10–12

❈ Preheat an oven to 400°F (200°C).

❈ Rinse the chicken pieces and pat dry with paper towels. Trim the excess fat from the prosciutto, then cut the slices to the dimensions of the chicken pieces.

❈ Carefully slide your fingers under the skin on each chicken piece, separating it from the meat but leaving it attached on one side. Place a slice of prosciutto directly on the meat and top it with a sage leaf. Carefully pull the skin back in place, and press gently with your palm to secure it.

❈ Arrange the chicken pieces in 1 or 2 shallow baking dishes or in a roasting pan large enough to hold them in a single layer. Brush the skin with the olive oil, and season with salt and pepper.

❈ Roast until the skin is crispy brown and the juices run clear when a thigh is pierced at the thickest part with a fork, about 55 minutes. Remove from the oven and let rest for 10 minutes before serving.

❈ Transfer the chicken pieces to a warmed platter and garnish with sage sprigs. Serve immediately.

NUTRITIONAL ANALYSIS PER SERVING: Calories 277 (Kilojoules 1,163); Protein 34 g; Carbohydrates 0 g; Total Fat 15 g; Saturated Fat 4 g; Cholesterol 0 mg; Sodium 279 mg; Dietary Fiber 0 g

Summer Vegetables and Caponata with Polenta

PREP TIME: 30 MINUTES

COOKING TIME: 1½ HOURS,
   PLUS 2 HOURS FOR
   CHILLING

INGREDIENTS

FOR THE CAPONATA

1 large eggplant (aubergine), about
   1½ lb (750 g), halved lengthwise

about ½ cup (4 fl oz/125 ml) olive oil

1 large white onion, chopped

1 tablespoon coarse salt

1½ teaspoons ground pepper

1 tablespoon extra-virgin olive oil

½ cup (¾ oz/20 g) chopped fresh
   flat-leaf (Italian) parsley

FOR THE POLENTA

4 cups (32 fl oz/1 l) water

1 cup (5 oz/155 g) stone-ground
   yellow cornmeal

2 teaspoons salt

1 tablespoon unsalted butter

FOR THE ROASTED VEGETABLES

2 each zucchini (courgettes) and
   yellow summer squashes, cut
   lengthwise into eighths

1 large red (Spanish) onion, cut
   through stem end into eighths

3 bell peppers (capsicums), 1 each
   green, yellow, and red, seeded
   and cut lengthwise into eighths

about 2 tablespoons olive oil

2 tablespoons chopped fresh basil

¼ cup (⅓ oz/10 g) minced fresh
   flat-leaf (Italian) parsley

SERVES 8

❈ To make the caponata, position a rack in the upper third of an oven and preheat to 450°F (230°C). Line a large baking pan with aluminum foil. Place the eggplant, cut sides down, on the prepared pan, and prick the skin with a fork in several places. Add a little water to the pan bottom to moisten. Roast until quite soft to the touch, about 45 minutes. Scoop out the warm pulp from the skin onto a cutting board; discard the skin. Cut into small cubes and transfer to a large nonaluminum bowl.

❈ Meanwhile, in a large frying pan over medium heat, warm the olive oil. Add the onion and sauté until soft, about 8 minutes. Add the eggplant and sauté, stirring occasionally and adding more oil if necessary to prevent scorching, until the vegetables are tender, about 5 minutes. Season with coarse salt and pepper. It should taste quite salty at this point. Transfer to a nonaluminum container. Pour the extra-virgin olive oil on top to cover completely, cover, and chill thoroughly, at least 2 hours.

❈ Meanwhile, make the polenta: Oil a rimmed baking sheet. In a saucepan over medium heat, bring 3 cups (24 fl oz/750 ml) of the water to a boil. In a bowl, whisk together the remaining 1 cup (8 fl oz/250 ml) of the water, the cornmeal, and salt. Whisk the cornmeal mixture into the boiling water until it returns to a boil. Reduce the heat to low and cook, stirring every 10 minutes, until thick and creamy, about 40 minutes. If it becomes too thick, add a little more water. Stir in the butter and spread evenly on the prepared sheet. Cover and chill for at least 1 hour to set.

❈ To roast the vegetables, preheat an oven to 425°F (220°C). Line 2 or 3 rimmed baking sheets with aluminum foil and brush with olive oil. Keeping the vegetables separate, arrange them in a single layer on the baking sheets. Drizzle with a few drops of olive oil, and then scatter with the basil. Roast until tender and crisp on the edges, 20–30 minutes. Keep warm.

❈ Cut the polenta into 24 diamonds. Spray a stove-top grill pan or heavy frying pan with nonstick cooking spray and warm over high heat. Add the polenta and grill, turning once, until crisp on the edges, about 4 minutes on each side. Stir the chopped parsley into the caponata. Spoon a mound of caponata in the center of each individual plate. Surround with 3 polenta triangles and some roasted vegetables. Dust with minced parsley. Serve warm or at room temperature.

NUTRITIONAL ANALYSIS PER SERVING: Calories 327 (Kilojoules 1,373); Protein 5 g; Carbohydrates 32 g; Total Fat 21 g; Saturated Fat 4 g; Cholesterol 4 mg; Sodium 1,149 mg; Dietary Fiber 5 g

Chicken-and-Apple Sausages with Mustard Sauce

PREP TIME: 5 MINUTES

COOKING TIME: 30 MINUTES

INGREDIENTS

4 smoked chicken-and-apple
   sausages, or other fruit-flavored
   chicken or turkey sausages, 3–4 oz
   (90–125 g) each

1 large Vidalia or red (Spanish)
   onion, sliced

½–¾ cup (4–6 fl oz/125–180 ml)
   full-bodied red wine

FOR THE MUSTARD SAUCE
3 oz (90 g) cream cheese

6 tablespoons (3 oz/90 g) Dijon
   mustard

½ teaspoon dry mustard, or to taste

STORAGE TIP: Store any leftover
mustard sauce, covered, in the refrigerator for up to 1 month. Serve with
sandwiches or other roasted meats.

In this simple dish, the flavor of the sausages is enhanced when
they are roasted atop onions and red wine, then slathered with
a creamy mustard sauce. Serve thick slices of coarse country
bread and crisp apple slices on the side.

SERVES 4

❀ Preheat an oven to 425°F (220°C).

❀ Using a sharp knife, slit each sausage in 3 or 4 places. Scatter the onion
slices in a 9-inch (23-cm) baking dish or pie dish. Place the sausages
directly on the onions, and pour ½ cup (4 fl oz/125 ml) of the wine into
the dish.

❀ Roast, adding more wine if necessary to prevent scorching, until the
sausages are browned and crisp, the onions are soft, and the wine is
nearly evaporated, 25–30 minutes.

❀ Meanwhile, make the mustard sauce: In a small, heatproof bowl set
over (but not touching) barely simmering water, stir the cream cheese
until warm and smooth. Remove from the heat and whisk in the Dijon
mustard and the ½ teaspoon dry mustard. Taste and add more dry mustard as needed. Transfer the mustard sauce to a small bowl.

❀ Serve the sausages and onions directly from the baking dish. Pass the
sauce at the table.

NUTRITIONAL ANALYSIS PER SERVING: Calories 336 (Kilojoules 1,411); Protein 19 g;
Carbohydrates 16 g; Total Fat 19 g; Saturated Fat 8 g; Cholesterol 35 mg; Sodium 1,132 mg;
Dietary Fiber 2 g

Pressed Chicken Breasts with Dried Cherries

PREP TIME: 20 MINUTES, PLUS
2 HOURS FOR MARINATING

COOKING TIME: 25 MINUTES,
PLUS 20 MINUTES FOR
RESTING

INGREDIENTS

8 skinless, boneless chicken breast
halves, 6–7 oz (185–220 g) each

I cup (4 oz/125 g) pitted dried
sweet cherries

2 large shallots, minced

¼ cup (2 fl oz/60 ml) lemon juice

3 tablespoons olive oil

grated zest of ½ lemon

½ teaspoon dried summer savory

½ teaspoon dried thyme

½ teaspoon coarse salt, or to taste

½ teaspoon ground pepper, or
to taste

fresh flat-leaf (Italian) parsley sprigs

COOKING TIP: Use 2 large glass baking dishes that are the same size (for
example, 9 by 13 inches/23 by 33 cm)
or 4 large pie dishes for pressing the
chicken.

Pressing the meat during and after roasting intensifies the sweet-tart nature of the cherry-stuffed chicken breasts. Their pretty red centers are revealed when the slices are arranged on a platter.

SERVES 6–8

❀ Working with 1 chicken breast half at a time, place the meat flat on a cutting board. Holding the meat firmly in place, use a small, sharp knife to cut a horizontal slit down 1 side and through the center of the meat, leaving 3 sides uncut.

❀ Spoon one-eighth of the dried cherries into each pocket. Firmly press on each breast with your hand to flatten the meat and seal the edges together. Arrange in a single layer in a nonaluminum dish.

❀ In a small bowl, stir together the shallots, lemon juice, olive oil, lemon zest, summer savory, thyme, salt, and pepper. Spoon the shallot mixture evenly over the chicken breasts. Cover and refrigerate for at least 2 hours or for up to 24 hours.

❀ Preheat a broiler (griller). Transfer the chicken to a broiler pan, reserving the marinade, and place under the broiler about 4 inches (10 cm) from the heat source. Broil (grill) until the meat is browned on top, 4–5 minutes.

❀ While the chicken is browning, pour the reserved marinade into a small saucepan over high heat. Bring to a boil and remove from the heat.

❀ Remove the chicken from the broiler. Set the oven at 375°F (190°C). Transfer the chicken pieces to a shallow baking dish large enough to hold them in a single layer. Pour the marinade over the meat, and set another baking dish directly on top of the meat. Roast until the juices run clear when the meat is pierced at the thickest point, 15–20 minutes.

❀ Remove from the oven and set 2 or 3 heavy cans or 1 or 2 bricks in the top (empty) baking dish to weight it down. Let rest for at least 20 minutes or for up to 30 minutes before serving.

❀ Transfer the chicken to a cutting board, and cut across the grain into slices. Arrange on a warmed platter, revealing the cherry stuffing. Spoon the dish juices over the top. Garnish with parsley.

NUTRITIONAL ANALYSIS PER SERVING: Calories 331 (Kilojoules 1,390); Protein 49 g; Carbohydrates 13 g; Total Fat 8 g; Saturated Fat 1 g; Cholesterol 122 mg; Sodium 246 mg; Dietary Fiber 0 g

Lobster with Cognac Butter

PREP TIME: 5 MINUTES

COOKING TIME: 20 MINUTES

INGREDIENTS

4 lobsters, split in half lengthwise
and cleaned

2 lemons, cut into wedges

¼–⅓ cup (2–3 fl oz/60–80 ml) cognac

leaves from 3 or 4 fresh tarragon
sprigs, minced

2 tablespoons unsalted butter, melted,
plus 6 tablespoons (3 oz/90 g)
unsalted butter

ground pepper to taste

about ⅓ cup (⅓ oz/10 g) minced
mixed fresh herbs such as
tarragon, chives, and flat-leaf
(Italian) parsley

PREP TIP: Have the fishmonger split
and clean the lobsters for you, and
then they can go directly into the
oven to roast. This eliminates any
apprehension you might have about
dealing with the live crustaceans.

Lobster doesn't have to be reserved for special occasions. Here,
a simple preparation can make any day feel like a celebration.

SERVES 4

❀ Preheat an oven to 425°F (220°C). Line 2 rimmed baking sheets with
aluminum foil. Arrange the lobster halves crosswise on the sheets, split
sides up. Squeeze the juice of 1 lemon over the lobsters and drizzle with
about 1 tablespoon cognac. Sprinkle with the minced tarragon leaves,
then brush with the melted butter.

❀ Roast the lobsters until the claw and tail meat is opaque, 14–16 minutes. Transfer the lobsters to warmed large individual plates, and tent
with aluminum foil to keep warm.

❀ Pour about ¼ cup (2 fl oz/60 ml) cognac into the pans and stir with a
wooden spoon to deglaze them, then pour all the liquid from the pans
into a small frying pan. Place the frying pan over high heat. Using a long
match, carefully ignite the cognac, then gently tilt the pan back and forth
until the flames subside and only a few tablespoons of liquid remain.
Working quickly, whisk the 6 tablespoons (3 oz/90 g) butter, 1 tablespoon
at a time, into the pan juices until the mixture becomes a creamy sauce.
Season with pepper and about ¼ cup (⅓ oz/10 g) of the minced herbs.
Taste and adjust the seasonings.

❀ Spoon the cognac butter into 4 small ramekins and set a ramekin
on each plate alongside the lobster. Dividing them evenly, scatter the
remaining minced herbs over each serving. Pass the remaining lemon
wedges at the table.

NUTRITIONAL ANALYSIS PER SERVING: Calories 332 (Kilojoules 1,394); Protein 31 g;
Carbohydrates 3 g; Total Fat 18 g; Saturated Fat 11 g; Cholesterol 154 mg; Sodium 572 mg;
Dietary Fiber 0 g

Mint-and-Chive–Marinated Leg of Lamb

PREP TIME: 30 MINUTES, PLUS
6 HOURS FOR MARINATING

COOKING TIME: 1¼ HOURS

INGREDIENTS

1 leg of lamb, 5–6 lb (2.5–3 kg), trimmed of fat

15–20 fresh mint sprigs

2 large cloves garlic, minced

12–16 ramps, chopped (see note)

½ bunch fresh chives, cut into 2-inch (5-cm) lengths

1 teaspoon peppercorns

2 cups (16 fl oz/500 ml) full-bodied white wine

coarse salt and ground pepper to taste

1–2 teaspoons olive oil, or as needed

2 green (spring) onions, coarsely chopped

3 celery stalks with leaves, coarsely chopped

Ramps, wild onions with a garlicky accent, are a harbinger of spring. If you cannot find them in the market, substitute 6 green (spring) onions and 1 garlic clove, chopping them together.

SERVES 8–10

❀ Make 15–20 small slits at regular intervals in the lamb. Remove 15–20 small leaves from the mint sprigs and insert into the slits. Bruise 6–8 of the mint sprigs. Place the lamb in a large, nonaluminum dish. Add the garlic, half of the ramps, the chives, the bruised mint sprigs, the peppercorns, and 1 cup (8 fl oz/250 ml) of the wine; turn the meat to coat evenly. Cover and refrigerate for at least 6 hours or for up to 3 days, turning occasionally. Bring to room temperature before roasting.

❀ Preheat an oven to 450°F (230°C). Remove the meat from the marinade and pat dry with paper towels. Pour the marinade into a small saucepan, bring to a boil, then remove from the heat. Rub the lamb with salt and ground pepper. In a roasting pan over high heat, warm enough olive oil to form a film on the pan bottom. Add the lamb and brown on all sides, 5–6 minutes total. Remove the lamb from the pan. Add the green onions, the remaining ramps, a sprig or two of mint, and the celery to the roasting pan. Set the lamb on top of the vegetables.

❀ Roast for 15 minutes. Reduce the temperature to 375°F (190°C) and continue to roast, basting every 10–15 minutes with the reserved marinade, until an instant-read thermometer inserted into the thickest portion of the leg away from the bone registers 125°–130°F (52°–54°C) for rosy- to medium-rare, about 35 minutes longer. Alternatively, cut into the meat with a sharp knife; it should be pink or done to your liking. Transfer to a cutting board, loosely tent with aluminum foil, and let rest for 10 minutes before carving.

❀ Meanwhile, place the pan over high heat. Add the remaining 1 cup (8 fl oz/250 ml) wine and deglaze the pan, stirring to remove any browned bits from the pan bottom. Bring to a boil and boil until reduced by one-half, 5–8 minutes. Spoon off the fat from the pan juices, then strain through a fine-mesh sieve into a warmed sauceboat.

❀ Carve across the grain into thin slices. Arrange on a warmed platter and garnish with the remaining mint sprigs. Pass the pan juices.

NUTRITIONAL ANALYSIS PER SERVING: Calories 245 (Kilojoules 1,029); Protein 37 g; Carbohydrates 3 g; Total Fat 9 g; Saturated Fat 3 g; Cholesterol 114 mg; Sodium 127 mg; Dietary Fiber 1 g

Roasted Fish Fillets with Tomato Salsa

PREP TIME: 25 MINUTES

COOKING TIME: 25 MINUTES

INGREDIENTS

FOR THE TOMATO SALSA

1 bunch fresh flat-leaf (Italian) parsley, tough stems removed

8–10 large fresh basil leaves, or to taste

3 or 4 fresh oregano sprigs, tough stems removed

1 teaspoon red pepper flakes

1 large Vidalia or other sweet onion, chopped

10 oil-packed sun-dried tomato halves, drained

3 large, firm ripe tomatoes, peeled and seeded

¼ cup (2 oz/60 g) small capers

coarse salt and freshly ground black pepper to taste

about 2 tablespoons extra-virgin olive oil

3 large Vidalia or other sweet onions, chopped

2 weakfish, sea bass, or red snapper fillets with skin intact, about 1¼ lb (625 g) each

salt and ground black pepper to taste

4 large fresh basil leaves, chopped

1 fresh oregano sprig, leaves only, chopped, or to taste

juice of ½ lemon

about 1 tablespoon olive oil

The juices from the tomato salsa mingle with the fish as it roasts to create an exquisite Mediterranean-style main course, ideal for late summer, when good tomatoes are plentiful.

SERVES 6

❋ To make the salsa, on a cutting board, coarsely chop the parsley. Add the basil, oregano, and red pepper flakes and continue to chop until finely chopped. Transfer to a bowl and add the onion. Working on the same board, mince the sun-dried tomatoes. Add the fresh tomatoes and continue chopping until evenly chopped. Transfer the tomatoes and their accumulated juices to the onion mixture, stir in the capers, and mix well. Season with salt and pepper, then add enough olive oil to bind the salsa lightly. Taste and adjust the seasonings. Set aside.

❋ Preheat an oven to 425°F (220°C). Lightly oil a baking dish large enough to hold the fillets in a single layer.

❋ Scatter the onions in the bottom of the dish. Rinse the fish fillets, pat dry with paper towels, and place, skin sides down, directly on the onions. Season with salt and pepper. Sprinkle the fillets with the basil and oregano, and then drizzle with the lemon juice and olive oil.

❋ Roast until the fish is half-cooked, 10–11 minutes. Spoon 3–4 tablespoons of the salsa with its juices directly over the fillets. Return the fillets to the oven and continue to roast until the fish is opaque throughout when pierced with a knife, 9–10 minutes longer.

❋ Transfer the remaining salsa to a small serving bowl. Serve the fish directly from the baking dish. Pass the salsa at the table.

NUTRITIONAL ANALYSIS PER SERVING: Calories 396 (Kilojoules 1,663); Protein 41 g; Carbohydrates 31 g; Total Fat 13 g; Saturated Fat 2 g; Cholesterol 78 mg; Sodium 471 mg; Dietary Fiber 6 g

Eye of Round with Vegetables

PREP TIME: 25 MINUTES, PLUS
24 HOURS FOR MARINATING

COOKING TIME: 2½ HOURS

INGREDIENTS

FOR THE MARINADE

1 bottle (24 fl oz/750 ml) full-bodied
  red wine

½ cup (4 fl oz/125 ml) cognac

5 large cloves garlic, chopped

1 yellow onion, chopped

1 bay leaf

3 or 4 fresh rosemary sprigs

½ teaspoon peppercorns

½ teaspoon whole cloves

1 eye of round beef roast, 4½–5 lb
  (2.25–2.5 kg)

coarse salt and ground pepper
  to taste

1½ cups (12 fl oz/375 ml) beef broth

8–10 cloves garlic, unpeeled

6 small onions, each 2 inches (5 cm)
  in diameter, peeled but left whole

3 turnips, peeled and quartered

3 large carrots, peeled and cut into
  2-inch (5-cm) chunks

3 parsnips, peeled and cut into 2-inch
  (5-cm) chunks

6 Yukon Gold or other yellow-
  fleshed potatoes, cut lengthwise
  into sixths

Ask the butcher to tie pieces of fat back (the unsalted, unsmoked fat layer that runs along a pig's back) onto the eye of round to help keep it moist and enrich its flavor as it roasts.

SERVES 10–12

❀ To make the marinade, in a large nonaluminum bowl, combine the wine, cognac, chopped garlic and onion, bay leaf, and rosemary. Tie the peppercorns and cloves in a piece of cheesecloth (muslin) and add to the bowl. Add the meat, turning to coat. Cover and refrigerate for at least 24 hours or for up to 2 days, turning occasionally.

❀ Preheat an oven to 400°F (200°C). Remove the meat from the marinade, pat dry with paper towels, and season with coarse salt and pepper. Strain the marinade and reserve the onion and garlic in one bowl and the liquid in another. Discard the remaining solids.

❀ Place a large dutch oven over high heat. Add the roast and brown on all sides, 7–8 minutes total. Transfer to a plate. Add the onion and garlic from the marinade to the pan and sauté for 1–2 minutes. Then add the marinade liquid and bring to a boil. Boil for 3–4 minutes, skimming off any scum. Return the meat to the dutch oven and add the broth and the whole garlic cloves. Roast, uncovered, until the meat is evenly browned on top, about 15 minutes. Reduce the temperature to 375°F (190°C), cover, and continue to roast for 1 hour.

❀ Meanwhile, cut a cross ¼ inch (6 mm) deep in the stem end of each whole onion to keep them from telescoping. When the meat has roasted for a total of 1¼ hours, arrange the onions, turnips, carrots, parsnips, and potatoes around it. Cover and continue to roast until the meat and vegetables are tender when pierced, about 1 hour longer.

❀ Transfer the meat to a cutting board and loosely tent with aluminum foil. Let rest for 5–8 minutes. Transfer the vegetables to a bowl and loosely tent with aluminum foil. Spoon off the fat from the pan juices.

❀ Snip the strings and discard any fat back that remains on the roast. Cut across the grain into thin slices and arrange on a warmed platter. Arrange the vegetables around the meat. Drizzle some of the pan juices over the meat and vegetables. Pass the remaining juices at the table.

NUTRITIONAL ANALYSIS PER SERVING: Calories 492 (Kilojoules 2,066); Protein 43 g; Carbohydrates 36 g; Total Fat 19 g; Saturated Fat 7 g; Cholesterol 103 mg; Sodium 7 mg; Dietary Fiber 6 g

Herbed Ricotta–Stuffed Chicken Breasts

PREP TIME: 25 MINUTES

COOKING TIME: 1 HOUR

INGREDIENTS

FOR THE STUFFING

2 tablespoons olive oil

2 large shallots, minced

3 large fresh mushrooms, brushed
    clean and chopped

1 cup (8 oz/250 g) whole-milk ricotta
    cheese

¼ cup (⅓ oz/10 g) minced fresh
    flat-leaf (Italian) parsley

2 tablespoons snipped fresh chives

2 teaspoons chopped fresh tarragon

coarse salt and ground pepper
    to taste

2 pinches of freshly grated nutmeg

6 boneless chicken breast halves,
    6–7 oz (185–220 g) each, with
    skin intact

about 1 teaspoon olive oil

coarse salt and ground pepper
    to taste

½ cup (4 fl oz/125 ml) chicken broth
    or dry white wine

fresh flat-leaf (Italian) parsley sprigs

MAKE-AHEAD TIP: The stuffing can
be made up to 4 days in advance.
Transfer to a clean container, press
plastic wrap directly onto the mixture, cover, and refrigerate.

For a more healthful main course, substitute low-fat ricotta cheese for the whole-milk cheese. Use any leftover stuffing in another chicken recipe, stuffed into slits in thick pork chops, or rolled up in veal scallops.

SERVES 6

❊ To make the stuffing, in a small sauté pan over medium heat, warm the olive oil. Add the shallots and sauté until they begin to soften, 1–2 minutes. Add the mushrooms and continue to sauté, stirring occasionally, until the mushrooms are tender, about 4 minutes. Let cool.

❊ Meanwhile, in a small bowl, stir together the cheese, minced parsley, chives, and tarragon until well mixed. Stir in the cooled shallot mixture, then season with salt, pepper, and nutmeg. Taste and adjust the seasonings.

❊ Preheat an oven to 425°F (220°C).

❊ Rinse the chicken breasts and pat dry with paper towels. Carefully slide your fingers under the skin on each breast, separating it from the meat but leaving it attached on one side. Spoon about 1½ tablespoons stuffing directly onto the meat and pull the skin back in place, covering the filling. Flatten the filling by gently pressing on the skin. Arrange the stuffed breasts in a roasting pan large enough to hold them in a single layer. Brush with the olive oil, and season with salt and pepper.

❊ Roast for 15 minutes. Reduce the oven temperature to 375°F (190°C). Continue to roast, basting every 10 minutes with the pan juices, until the skin is crispy brown and the juices run clear when the meat is pierced at the thickest point with a fork, about 30 minutes longer.

❊ Transfer the chicken to a plate and keep warm. Place the roasting pan over high heat. Add the broth or wine and deglaze the pan, stirring to remove any browned bits from the pan bottom. Bring to a boil and boil until reduced by one-half, about 5 minutes. Spoon off the fat from the pan juices, then strain through a fine-mesh sieve into a warmed sauceboat.

❊ Arrange each chicken breast on an individual plate. Garnish with parsley sprigs. Serve immediately. Pass the pan juices at the table.

NUTRITIONAL ANALYSIS PER SERVING: Calories 371 (Kilojoules 1,558); Protein 42 g; Carbohydrates 3 g; Total Fat 20 g; Saturated Fat 7 g; Cholesterol 125 mg; Sodium 208 mg; Dietary Fiber 1 g

Butterflied Leg of Lamb Provençal

PREP TIME: 30 MINUTES, PLUS
3 HOURS FOR MARINATING

COOKING TIME: 1¼ HOURS

INGREDIENTS

1 leg of lamb, 5–6 lb (2.5–3 kg),
   trimmed of fat, boned, and
   butterflied

7 large cloves garlic

coarse salt and ground pepper
   to taste

1 bottle (24 fl oz/750 ml) full-bodied
   red wine

9 oil-packed sun-dried tomatoes,
   drained

½ cup (2½ oz/75 g) pitted oil-cured
   olives, plus extra for garnish

2 tablespoons herbes de Provence

2 teaspoons freshly ground pepper

1–2 teaspoons olive oil, or as needed

chopped fresh flat-leaf (Italian)
   parsley

MAKE-AHEAD TIP: The seasoning
paste can be made up to 1 week
ahead. Place in a container, pour a
film of olive oil over the surface, cover
tightly, and store in the refrigerator.

SERVES 8–10

❀ Make 15–20 small slits at regular intervals in the butterflied lamb. Sliver 2 of the garlic cloves, and insert into the slits. Season the meat with salt and pepper. Place the lamb in a large lock-top plastic bag or a nonaluminum dish, and add 2 cups (16 fl oz/500 ml) of the wine. Seal the bag securely, or cover the dish. Refrigerate for at least 3 hours or for up to 3 days, turning occasionally. Bring to room temperature before roasting.

❀ On a cutting board, place the remaining 5 garlic cloves, sprinkle with a few pinches of coarse salt, then chop. Add the sun-dried tomatoes, ½ cup (2½ oz/75 g) olives, herbes de Provence, and pepper, and continue to chop to form a coarse paste.

❀ Preheat an oven to 450°F (230°C). Remove the lamb from the marinade and lay it flat, cut side up. Pour the marinade into a small saucepan, bring to a boil, and remove from the heat. Evenly spread the tomato-olive paste over the meat. Roll up the lamb and tie securely with kitchen string at intervals of 2–3 inches (5–7.5 cm).

❀ In a roasting pan over high heat, warm enough olive oil to form a film on the pan bottom. Add the lamb and brown on all sides, 5–6 minutes total. Transfer to the oven and roast for 15 minutes. Reduce the oven temperature to 350°F (180°C) and continue to roast, basting every 10–15 minutes with the reserved marinade, until an instant-read thermometer inserted into the thickest portion registers 125°–130°F (52°–54°C) for rosy- to medium-rare, about 45 minutes. Alternatively, cut into the meat with a sharp knife; it should be pink or done to your liking. Transfer to a cutting board, loosely tent with aluminum foil, and let rest for 10 minutes before carving.

❀ Meanwhile, place the roasting pan over high heat. Add 1 cup (8 fl oz/ 250 ml) of the wine and deglaze the pan, stirring to dislodge any browned bits from the pan bottom. Bring to a boil and boil until reduced by one-half, 5–8 minutes. Spoon off the fat from the pan juices, then strain through a fine-mesh sieve into a warmed sauceboat.

❀ Snip the strings and carve the lamb across the grain into thin slices. Arrange on a warmed platter, sprinkle with chopped parsley, and garnish with the olives. Pass the pan juices at the table.

NUTRITIONAL ANALYSIS PER SERVING: Calories 291 (Kilojoules 1,222); Protein 38 g; Carbohydrates 5 g; Total Fat 13 g; Saturated Fat 3 g; Cholesterol 114 mg; Sodium 405 mg; Dietary Fiber 1 g

Veal Stuffed with Spring Greens

SERVES 6–8

PREP TIME: 45 MINUTES, PLUS
3 HOURS FOR MARINATING

COOKING TIME: 1¾ HOURS

INGREDIENTS

1 boneless veal roast cut from the
leg, 4 lb (2 kg), trimmed of fat

4 cups (32 fl oz/1 l) milk

ground pepper to taste

freshly grated nutmeg to taste

FOR THE STUFFING

1 cup (1 oz/30 g) arugula (rocket)
leaves, tough stems removed

1 cup (1 oz/30 g) mâche leaves

1 cup (1 oz/30 g) watercress leaves,
tough stems removed

½ bunch fresh flat-leaf (Italian)
parsley, tough stems removed

2 tablespoons unsalted butter

2 tablespoons olive oil, or as needed

2 large shallots, minced

1 bunch fresh chives, minced

2 cups (2 oz/60 g) baby spinach
leaves, tough stems removed

freshly grated nutmeg to taste

coarse salt and ground pepper
to taste

about 18 green (spring) onions,
including 1 inch (2.5 cm) of green,
coarsely chopped

½ cup (4 fl oz/125 ml) dry white wine

½ cup (4 fl oz/125 ml) veal stock or
chicken broth

watercress sprigs

❀ Place the veal in a large, heavy-duty lock-top bag or a shallow nonaluminum dish. Pour the milk over the meat and turn to coat well. Seal the bag or cover the dish and refrigerate for at least 3 hours or for up to 24 hours. Discard the milk, rinse the roast, and pat dry with paper towels. Using a sharp knife, make a horizontal cut through the center of the meat and open it out flat. Generously rub with pepper and nutmeg. Bring to room temperature, about 30 minutes.

❀ Meanwhile, make the stuffing: In a food processor, combine the arugula, mâche, watercress, and parsley and pulse to chop evenly but coarsely. In a large sauté pan over medium heat, melt the butter with 1 tablespoon of the oil. Add the shallots and sauté until soft, about 3 minutes. Add the chives and sauté until soft, about 1 minute longer. Add all of the chopped greens and sauté, tossing constantly, for 1 minute. Add the whole spinach leaves and continue to sauté until wilted, about 2 minutes longer. Season with nutmeg, salt, and pepper. Mix well, then taste and adjust the seasonings. Let cool completely.

❀ Preheat an oven to 400°F (200°C). Spread the stuffing over the cut side of the meat, then roll up to enclose. Using kitchen string, tie securely at intervals 2–3 inches (5–7.5 cm) apart. Place a dutch oven over high heat and add the remaining olive oil as needed to form a film on the pan bottom. Add the veal and brown quickly on all sides, 4–5 minutes total. Scatter the green onions around the meat, cover, and roast for 20 minutes.

❀ Meanwhile, in a small saucepan, bring the wine and stock to a simmer. Remove from the heat. After the roast has been cooking for 20 minutes, pour the hot wine mixture over the meat. Reduce the oven temperature to 350°F (180°C) and continue to cook, covered, basting every 10 minutes, until the juices run rosy yellow when the meat is pierced at the thickest point, or an instant-read thermometer inserted into the thickest point registers 165°F (74°C), about 1 hour longer. Transfer to a cutting board, tent with aluminum foil, and let rest for 15 minutes before carving.

❀ Spoon off the fat from the pan juices. Boil until reduced by one-half, about 8 minutes. Taste and adjust the seasonings. Strain through a fine-mesh sieve into a warmed bowl. Slice the meat across the grain. Arrange on a warmed platter and garnish with watercress. Pass the pan juices.

NUTRITIONAL ANALYSIS PER SERVING: Calories 365 (Kilojoules 1,533); Protein 57 g; Carbohydrates 5 g; Total Fat 12 g; Saturated Fat 12 g; Cholesterol 211 mg; Sodium 264 mg; Dietary Fiber 2 g

Cornish Hens au Poivre

PREP TIME: 25 MINUTES, PLUS
1 HOUR FOR MARINATING

COOKING TIME: 40 MINUTES

INGREDIENTS

FOR THE SPICED PEPPERCORNS

3 tablespoons mixed peppercorns

¼ teaspoon red pepper flakes

8 whole allspice

8 juniper berries

6 Cornish hens, 2–2½ lb (1–1.25 kg) each

1 tablespoon coarse salt

3–4 tablespoons olive oil

juice of 2 lemons

watercress sprigs

This unusual spice mixture possesses a unique peppery base that penetrates through the skin during the dry marinating time and then seasons the hens more fully during roasting.

SERVES 6

❀ To make the spiced peppercorns, in a bowl, stir together the peppercorns, red pepper flakes, allspice, and juniper berries. Transfer to a pepper mill or spice grinder and grind coarsely. Set aside.

❀ At least 1 hour or up to 24 hours before roasting, rinse the hens and pat dry with paper towels. Using a sharp, heavy knife or kitchen shears, split each hen in half down the back and the breastbone. Tuck the leg into the skin, pushing it up to meet the breastbone, and fold back the wing of each hen half. Using the flat side of a cleaver, pound the skin side of each half to flatten the meat and facilitate even cooking. In a small bowl, combine the spiced peppercorns and the salt, and generously rub the entire surface of the hen halves with the mixture. Place the hen halves, skin sides up, in a shallow roasting pan large enough to hold them in a single layer. Let stand, uncovered, for 1 hour at room temperature or covered for up to 24 hours in the refrigerator. Bring to room temperature before roasting.

❀ Preheat an oven to 425°F (220°C).

❀ Arrange the hen halves, skin sides down, in the pan. Drizzle about ¼ teaspoon of the olive oil and ¼ teaspoon of the lemon juice over each half. Roast until the meat begins to brown, about 12 minutes. Turn over the birds and baste with the remaining oil and lemon juice. Continue to roast until the skin is crisp and browned and the juices run clear when the meat is pierced at the thickest point with a fork, or until an instant-read thermometer inserted into the thickest part of the thigh away from the bone registers 165°–170°F (74°–77°C), 25–30 minutes longer. Transfer the hens to a warmed platter and let rest for 5–10 minutes before serving.

❀ While the hens are resting, spoon off the fat from the pan juices. Strain the pan juices through a fine-mesh sieve into a warmed bowl and keep warm.

❀ Garnish the platter with watercress. Pass the pan juices at the table.

NUTRITIONAL ANALYSIS PER SERVING: Calories 1,189 (Kilojoules 4,994); Protein 97 g; Carbohydrates 3 g; Total Fat 85 g; Saturated Fat 23 g; Cholesterol 562 mg; Sodium 1,024 mg; Dietary Fiber 2 g

Pork Loin with Orange-Ginger Glaze

PREP TIME: 25 MINUTES, PLUS
4 HOURS FOR MARINATING

COOKING TIME: 1¾ HOURS

INGREDIENTS

2 boneless pork loins, 3–3½ lb
(1.5–1.75 kg) each, tied at 2-inch
(5-cm) intervals

2 large cloves garlic, slivered
(20–24 slivers)

8–10 tiny red chiles, slivered
(20–24 slivers)

1 teaspoon coarse salt

½ teaspoon ground pepper

¼ cup (2 fl oz/60 ml) olive oil

¼ cup (2 fl oz/60 ml) orange juice

FOR THE ORANGE-GINGER GLAZE

2 cups (1¼ lb/625 g) orange
marmalade

1 yellow onion, minced

2 slices fresh ginger, peeled and
minced

1 small clove garlic, minced

½ cup (4 fl oz/125 ml) orange juice

2–3 tablespoons Grand Marnier or
other orange liqueur

1 bunch fresh garlic chives, or
12 green (spring) onions, trimmed
but left whole

zest strips from ½ orange

Tiny, fiery hot Mexican chiles and slivers of garlic infuse the meat overnight; use more if you like your food spicy. You can roast potatoes, shallots, and root vegetables such as carrots and beets in the same pan, if you wish; cut them into 1½-inch (4-cm) pieces and add them one hour before the pork loin is done.

SERVES 10–12

❋ Using a small knife, make 20–24 small slits at regular intervals in each of the pork loins. Tuck a garlic sliver into half of the slits and a chile sliver into the other half, alternating them as you work. Rub the meat with the salt and pepper. Set each pork loin in a large nonaluminum pan. In a small bowl, whisk together the olive oil and orange juice and pour half over each loin. Cover and refrigerate for at least 4 hours or for up to 24 hours. Bring to room temperature before roasting.

❋ To make the glaze, in a small, heavy saucepan over medium heat, stir together the orange marmalade, onion, ginger, and garlic, and bring to a boil. Stir in the orange juice, reduce the heat to low, and simmer for 5 minutes. Stir in 2 tablespoons of the Grand Marnier, taste, and adjust the flavorings. Remove from the heat and set aside.

❋ Preheat an oven to 400°F (200°C). Remove the pork from the marinade and transfer to a large roasting pan. Pour the marinade into a small saucepan over high heat, bring to a boil, remove from the heat, and set aside. Place the roasting pan over high heat, add the pork, and brown on all sides, about 5 minutes. Lift the meat out of the pan, and place the garlic chives or green onions in the pan (reserve a few chives for garnish, if desired). Replace the meat and pour the hot marinade around the meat.

❋ Roast the pork, basting with the orange-ginger glaze every 10 minutes, until the meat is browned, glazed, and tender when pierced with a knife, or an instant-read thermometer registers 155°–160°F (68°–71°C), about 1½ hours. Transfer the meat to 1 or 2 cutting boards, loosely tent with aluminum foil, and let rest for 15 minutes before carving.

❋ Cut across the grain into thin slices, arrange on a warmed platter, and garnish with curls of orange zest and the reserved garlic chives, if desired. Reheat any remaining glaze and pass at the table.

NUTRITIONAL ANALYSIS PER SERVING: Calories 722 (Kilojoules 3,032); Protein 53 g; Carbohydrates 39 g; Total Fat 39 g; Saturated Fat 12 g; Cholesterol 169 mg; Sodium 298 mg; Dietary Fiber 0 g

Saffron-Scented Halibut with Spinach, Zucchini, and Tomato

PREP TIME: 20 MINUTES, PLUS
1 HOUR FOR MARINATING

COOKING TIME: 30 MINUTES

INGREDIENTS

2 lemons

3 tablespoons olive oil

pinch of saffron threads

6 halibut fillets, each 6–7 oz
(185–220 g) and about ¾ inch
(2 cm) thick, skinned

coarse salt and ground pepper
to taste

FOR THE VEGETABLES
3–4 tablespoons olive oil

3 large shallots, diced

⅛ teaspoon saffron threads

1 lb (500 g) spinach, tough stems
removed

coarse salt and ground pepper
to taste

3 or 4 small zucchini (courgettes),
diced

2 large tomatoes, peeled, seeded,
and diced

juice of 1 lemon

½ bunch fresh flat-leaf (Italian)
parsley, minced

Have plenty of coarse country bread on hand to soak up the
fragrant juices on the plate.

SERVES 6

❋ In a small bowl, whisk together the juice of 1 lemon, the olive oil, and
the saffron. Season the fish fillets with coarse salt and pepper. Place in
a nonaluminum dish in a single layer. Pour the oil mixture over the fish
and turn to coat. Cover and refrigerate for 1–2 hours.

❋ Preheat an oven to 450°F (230°C).

❋ Spray a roasting pan with nonstick cooking spray and place in the
oven until it is hot, about 5 minutes. Sprinkle a little coarse salt on the
bottom of the hot pan. Lift the fish fillets from the marinade, reserving
the marinade, and place them, skin sides down, on the hot pan. Roast
until opaque throughout when pierced with a knife, 7–10 minutes.

❋ Meanwhile, prepare the vegetables: In a large nonaluminum sauté pan
over medium-high heat, warm the olive oil. Add the shallots and sauté
until they begin to soften, 2–3 minutes. Add the saffron and continue to
cook until the shallots are soft, about 4 minutes longer. Transfer about
1 tablespoon of the shallots to a small dish and set aside.

❋ Raise the heat under the sauté pan to high. Working in 3 batches, add
the spinach leaves to the shallots remaining in the pan. Sauté, tossing
constantly, until the spinach is wilted but still bright green, 4–5 minutes.
Transfer to a plate, season with salt and pepper, and keep warm.

❋ Place the sauté pan over medium heat and add the reserved shallots.
Add the zucchini and cook, stirring occasionally, until it begins to soften,
2–3 minutes. Add the tomatoes and cook, stirring, until the tomatoes
begin to soften, 3–4 minutes. Add the reserved marinade, raise the heat
to high, and cook until the sauce is slightly thickened and the vegetables
are just tender, 5–7 minutes longer. Season with salt, pepper, and
lemon juice.

❋ Mound a portion of the spinach in the center of each individual plate.
Top each with a fish fillet, and spoon the zucchini mixture over the fish.
Dust the fish and the plate with the parsley. Cut the remaining lemon
into wedges, divide among the plates, and serve.

NUTRITIONAL ANALYSIS PER SERVING: Calories 379 (Kilojoules 1,592); Protein 42 g;
Carbohydrates 10 g; Total Fat 20 g; Saturated Fat 3 g; Cholesterol 59 mg; Sodium 153 mg;
Dietary Fiber 3 g

Provençal Roasted Turkey Breast

PREP TIME: 25 MINUTES

COOKING TIME: 2¾ HOURS

INGREDIENTS

1 carrot, peeled and chopped

1 celery stalk, chopped

2 small yellow onions, chopped

1 bone-in turkey breast, 5–6 lb
    (2.5–3 kg)

1 lemon, halved

coarse salt and ground pepper
    to taste

FOR THE SEASONING PASTE

4 shallots

1 generous cup (6 oz/185 g) pitted
    oil-cured black olives

1 tablespoon herbes de Provence

½ teaspoon ground pepper

½ cup (½ oz/15 g) firmly packed fresh
    flat-leaf (Italian) parsley leaves

1 tablespoon olive oil

8–10 Vidalia or other sweet onions

MAKE-AHEAD TIP: The seasoning
paste can be made 1 week in advance.
Transfer the paste to a clean container,
pour a thin film of olive oil over the
top, cover, and store in the refrigerator.

If there are leftovers, build a fabulous club sandwich with tomato, lettuce, bacon, and a slice or two of the turkey. Smear a little of the seasoning paste on the bread.

SERVES 8–10

❀ Preheat an oven to 400°F (200°C). Scatter the chopped carrot, celery, and 1 of the yellow onions in the bottom of a large roasting pan. Set a rack over the vegetables.

❀ Rinse the turkey breast and pat dry with paper towels. Rub the inside with the lemon, sprinkle with salt and pepper, and set aside.

❀ To make the seasoning paste, in a food processor, combine the shallots, olives, herbes de Provence, pepper, and parsley. Pulse until evenly chopped but not smooth; set aside.

❀ Carefully slide your fingers under the skin on the turkey breast, separating it from the flesh but leaving it attached on the sides. Spread the seasoning paste under the skin, in the wing sockets, and inside the cavity. Fill the cavity with the remaining chopped onion. Brush the skin with the olive oil and set the turkey breast, on one side, on the rack.

❀ Roast until the skin is browned, 15–20 minutes. Turn the breast onto the opposite side and continue to roast until the skin on the second side is browned, 15–20 minutes. Reduce the oven temperature to 350°F (180°C), turn the breast right side up, and continue to roast, basting every 10 minutes with the pan juices during the last 30 minutes, until the skin is crisp and browned and the juices run clear when the meat is pierced at the thickest portion with a fork, or until an instant-read thermometer registers 162°–165°F (72°–74°C), about 2 hours longer. If the turkey skin is browning too fast, tent with aluminum foil. Meanwhile, cut the onions as directed for Balsamic Vidalia Blossoms on page 89. Add the onions to the pan during the last 35–40 minutes and roast, basting with the pan juices as well, until tender.

❀ Transfer the turkey breast to a cutting board, loosely tent with aluminum foil, and let rest for 15 minutes before carving. Cut the turkey across the grain into thin slices, and arrange on a warmed platter. Garnish with the Vidalia onions and serve immediately.

NUTRITIONAL ANALYSIS PER SERVING: Calories 569 (Kilojoules 2,391); Protein 59 g; Carbohydrates 25 g; Total Fat 26 g; Saturated Fat 5 g; Cholesterol 163 mg; Sodium 799 mg; Dietary Fiber 4 g

Chicken with Garden Vegetables

INGREDIENTS

4 shallots

1 teaspoon unsalted butter, plus 1 tablespoon, at room temperature

coarse salt and ground pepper to taste

1 teaspoon fresh thyme leaves

3 carrots, peeled, sliced, blanched for 3 minutes, and drained

1 fennel bulb, trimmed, sliced cross-wise, blanched for 3 minutes, and drained

3 celery stalks, sliced, blanched for 3 minutes, and drained

2 cups (10 oz/310 g) English peas

1 large roasting chicken, 7–8 lb (3.5–4 kg), with neck and giblets reserved for another use

1 lemon, halved

about 1 cup (8 fl oz/250 ml) chicken broth

COOKING TIP: If the roasting pan is too small to hold the extra vegetables, place them in a separate baking dish and moisten with a spoonful or so of the pan juices. Roast until tender when pierced, about 30 minutes. You can also add 8 Yukon Gold potatoes, halved, to the roasting pan about 1 hour before the chicken is done.

SERVES 8

❋ Slice 2 of the shallots. In a small frying pan over medium heat, melt the 1 teaspoon butter. Add the sliced shallots and sauté until limp, 3–4 minutes. Transfer to a bowl and season with salt, pepper, and the thyme. Add half each of the blanched carrots, fennel, celery, and peas. Toss well. Taste and adjust the seasonings. In another bowl, toss together the remaining blanched vegetables and the remaining 1 cup (5 oz/155 g) peas. Quarter the remaining 2 shallots, add to the bowl, and toss again. Cover and set aside.

❋ Preheat an oven to 425°F (220°C). Rinse the chicken and pat dry with paper towels. Rub the cavity with the cut sides of the lemon, then sprinkle with coarse salt. Lightly spoon the seasoned vegetables into the main and neck cavities. Rub the remaining 1 tablespoon butter over and under the skin of the chicken, sliding your fingers between the skin and the flesh. Secure the neck cavity closed with toothpicks or small metal skewers. Cross the drumsticks and, using kitchen string, tie together. Place the stuffed chicken, breast side down, on a rack in a large roasting pan, tucking the wing tips underneath the breasts.

❋ Roast until the skin is brown on the back, 15–20 minutes. Reduce the oven temperature to 375°F (190°C). Turn the chicken breast side up and continue to roast, basting every 10 minutes with the pan juices during the last 30 minutes, until the skin is browned and the juices run clear, or an instant-read thermometer inserted into the thickest part of the thigh away from the bone registers 165°–170°F (74°–77°C), about 1½ hours longer. Scatter the reserved blanched vegetables around the chicken 30 minutes before it is done.

❋ Transfer the chicken to a cutting board and let rest for 15 minutes before carving. If the vegetables are not yet tender, continue to roast until tender. Using a slotted spoon, transfer the vegetables to a warmed bowl, then place the pan over high heat. Add the broth and deglaze the pan, stirring to remove any browned bits. Boil until reduced to about 1 cup (8 fl oz/250 ml), about 8 minutes. Adjust the seasonings. Spoon off the fat, then strain through a fine-mesh sieve into a warmed bowl.

❋ Remove the skewers and strings from the chicken. Spoon the stuffing into a warmed bowl. Carve the chicken. Pass the pan juices at the table.

NUTRITIONAL ANALYSIS PER SERVING: Calories 592 (Kilojoules 2,486); Protein 56 g; Carbohydrates 10 g; Total Fat 35 g; Saturated Fat 10 g; Cholesterol 175 mg; Sodium 349 mg; Dietary Fiber 3 g

Swiss-Style Steak

PREP TIME: 15 MINUTES, PLUS
12 HOURS FOR MARINATING

COOKING TIME: 1¼ HOURS

INGREDIENTS

1 top round steak, first cut, 3–3½ lb (1.5–1.75 kg) and 1½ inches (4 cm) thick

2 cups (16 fl oz/500 ml) tomato juice

1 tablespoon plus 2 teaspoons dried basil

1 teaspoon ground pepper, plus pepper to taste

6 cloves garlic, minced

2 yellow onions

coarse salt to taste

1 tablespoon olive oil, plus extra as needed

3 large tomatoes, seeded and chopped

½ bunch fresh flat-leaf (Italian) parsley, chopped, plus extra for garnish

2 pinches of sugar, or to taste

Here, round steak is tenderized in a marinade of tomato juice, then roasted on a bed of basil-scented onions and ripe tomatoes. The resulting tomato sauce has the character of a fresh salsa. Use the first cut of the top round, if possible, as it is the most tender. Lengthen the marinating and cooking times if using a less tender cut.

SERVES 6

❈ Place the steak in a large, heavy-duty lock-top plastic bag or a shallow nonaluminum dish. Add the tomato juice, 1 tablespoon basil, 1 teaspoon pepper, and 4 of the minced garlic cloves. Slice 1 of the onions and add it as well. Press out the air and seal the bag securely, or cover the dish. Refrigerate for at least 12 hours or for up to 24 hours, turning occasionally.

❈ Preheat an oven to 400°F (200°C).

❈ Remove the steak from the marinade, pat dry with paper towels, and season with salt and pepper. Discard the marinade.

❈ In a dutch oven over high heat, warm the 1 tablespoon olive oil. Add the meat and sear on both sides until browned, about 4 minutes on each side. Remove from the heat.

❈ Chop the remaining onion. In a saucepan over medium heat, warm as much olive oil as needed to form a film on the pan bottom. Add the chopped onion and the remaining garlic and sauté until the onion begins to soften, about 2 minutes. Add the tomatoes, 2 teaspoons basil, ½ bunch parsley, sugar, and salt and pepper to taste. Stir well and cook until the tomatoes begin to release their juices, 2–3 minutes. Remove from the heat and spoon the tomato mixture around the steak.

❈ Place the steak in the oven and roast, uncovered, until the meat is browned on top, about 25 minutes. Cover and continue to roast until the meat is tender, 25–30 minutes longer.

❈ Remove the meat from the oven and cut across the grain into thick slices. Arrange the slices on a warmed platter, spooning the tomato mixture alongside. Garnish with chopped parsley and serve immediately.

NUTRITIONAL ANALYSIS PER SERVING: Calories 501 (Kilojoules 2,104); Protein 55 g; Carbohydrates 11 g; Total Fat 26 g; Saturated Fat 9 g; Cholesterol 150 mg; Sodium 209 mg; Dietary Fiber 2 g

Smoky Southwestern Veal Chops

PREP TIME: 25 MINUTES, PLUS
3 HOURS FOR MARINATING

COOKING TIME: 30 MINUTES

INGREDIENTS

6 loin veal chops, each 6–7 oz
(185–220 g) and 1 inch (2.5 cm)
thick, trimmed of fat and edges
scored

2 chipotle chiles

about 2½ cups (20 fl oz/625 ml) milk

1 dried árbol chile

1 dried Anaheim chile

1 ancho chile

1 teaspoon coarse salt, plus a pinch

about 2 tablespoons vegetable oil

2 large cloves garlic, minced

1 large yellow onion, chopped

½ bunch fresh cilantro (fresh
coriander), tough stems removed
and leaves chopped

⅓ cup (3 fl oz/80 ml) veal stock or
chicken broth, warmed

1 cup (8 oz/250 g) hulled green
pumpkin seeds (see note)

Chipotle chiles, which are dried smoked jalapeños, have an almost chocolaty taste. Here, the chipotle imparts its unique character to veal chops before they are smeared with a hot seasoning paste. Hulled green pumpkin seeds, also known as *pepitas,* are sold in Mexican markets and health-food stores.

SERVES 6

❈ Place the veal chops and chipotle chiles in a large lock-top bag or dish. Pour in enough milk just to cover the meat. Seal the bag securely, or cover the dish. Refrigerate for at least 3 hours or for up to 24 hours. Discard the milk and chiles, rinse the chops, and pat dry with paper towels.

❈ Preheat an oven to 400°F (200°C).

❈ Using metal tongs, pass the remaining dried chiles one at a time over a flame on a gas stove to toast briefly, being careful not to blacken them. If using an electric stove, place the chiles, one at a time, in a nonstick frying pan over medium heat and toast quickly until aromatic, about 1 minute. Using a mortar and pestle, grind together all the toasted chiles with 1 teaspoon coarse salt until coarsely crushed. Rub the mixture into both sides of each chop and set aside.

❈ In a large frying pan over medium-high heat, warm the oil. Brown the chops, turning once, about 4 minutes on each side. Transfer to a plate. Reduce the heat to medium and add the garlic and onion. Cook, stirring often, until they begin to soften, about 6 minutes. Stir in the cilantro. Transfer the onion mixture to a baking dish large enough to hold the chops in a single layer. Place the chops, along with any accumulated juices, on the onions and pour the stock around the meat. Roast until tender and the juices run clear, 12–14 minutes.

❈ While the chops are roasting, place a small, dry frying pan over high heat. Toast the pumpkin seeds with a pinch of salt, shaking the pan constantly, until the seeds are lightly browned on the edges and begin to make a popping sound, 3–4 minutes. Transfer to paper towels and set aside.

❈ When the chops are ready, transfer them and the onions to a warmed platter. Sprinkle with the pumpkin seeds and serve immediately.

NUTRITIONAL ANALYSIS PER SERVING: Calories 393 (Kilojoules 1,651); Protein 32 g; Carbohydrates 12 g; Total Fat 26 g; Saturated Fat 5 g; Cholesterol 86 mg; Sodium 407 mg; Dietary Fiber 6 g

Roasted Salmon Fillets on Leeks and Fennel

PREP TIME: 20 MINUTES

COOKING TIME: 20 MINUTES

INGREDIENTS

3 fennel bulbs

4 or 5 large leeks, including 1 inch
(2.5 cm) of green, julienned

coarse salt and ground pepper
to taste

6 salmon fillets, 6–7 oz (185–220 g)
each, skinned

1 teaspoon fresh thyme leaves

juice of 1 lemon

2–3 tablespoons extra-virgin olive oil

In this fast and easy main course, the sweet licorice notes of the fennel and the subtle onion quality of the leeks marry well with the rich salmon. The recipe can be easily increased to serve additional guests.

SERVES 6

❊ Preheat an oven to 425°F (220°C). Lightly oil a rimmed baking sheet with olive oil.

❊ Cut off the stems and feathery tops and any bruised outer stalks from the fennel bulbs. Finely chop the tops of 1 bulb and reserve the tops of 1 of the other bulbs for garnish. Discard the remaining tops and any stems. Cut each bulb in half lengthwise and trim away the tough core. Cut the bulbs crosswise into thin slices.

❊ Scatter about one-half of the leeks and about one-half of the sliced fennel bulbs evenly over the bottom of the prepared baking sheet. Lightly season with salt and pepper. Place the salmon fillets, skin sides down, on top of the vegetables. Season with salt, pepper, half of the thyme, and about ¼ cup (⅓ oz/10 g) of the chopped fennel tops. Drizzle with half of the lemon juice and half of the olive oil.

❊ Roast the salmon until opaque throughout when pierced with a knife, about 20 minutes. The cooking time will depend upon the thickness of the fish; allow about 10 minutes for each inch (2.5 cm).

❊ Meanwhile, place the remaining chopped leeks and fennel in a baking dish. Season the vegetables with salt and pepper and the remaining thyme, chopped fennel tops, lemon juice, and olive oil. Roast the vegetables alongside the fish until the vegetables are lightly browned and tender, about 15 minutes.

❊ Using a spatula, transfer the salmon and vegetables to a warmed platter. Garnish with the reserved feathery fennel tops. Transfer the separately roasted vegetables to a warmed serving dish. Serve the fish and vegetables immediately.

NUTRITIONAL ANALYSIS PER SERVING: Calories 410 (Kilojoules 1,772); Protein 40 g; Carbohydrates 20 g; Total Fat 19 g; Saturated Fat 3 g; Cholesterol 101 mg; Sodium 256 mg; Dietary Fiber 3 g

Acorn Squash Stuffed with Wild Rice

PREP TIME: 20 MINUTES, PLUS
30 MINUTES FOR SOAKING

COOKING TIME: 1½ HOURS

INGREDIENTS

½ cup (3 oz/90 g) wild rice

4 cups (32 fl oz/1 l) water

1 teaspoon coarse salt, plus salt
to taste

10 dried shiitake mushrooms,
soaked in warm water to cover
for 30 minutes

3 large acorn squash, 2–2½ lb
(1–1.25 kg) each, halved lengthwise
and seeds and fibers discarded

1 tablespoon maple syrup, plus
about 1 teaspoon (optional)

2 tablespoons unsalted butter

1 tablespoon olive oil, or as needed

1 yellow onion, finely diced

1 celery stalk, finely diced

1 carrot, peeled and finely diced

1 tablespoon minced fresh marjoram
or 1 teaspoon dried marjoram

ground pepper to taste

1 tablespoon Madeira wine, or
to taste

½ cup (2 oz/60 g) pecan halves

The Madeira-flavored mixture of wild rice and shiitake mushrooms is irresistible when roasted in an acorn squash.

SERVES 6

❀ In a saucepan over high heat, combine the wild rice, water, and 1 teaspoon salt. Bring to a boil, reduce the heat to low, cover partially, and simmer until tender, about 45 minutes. Drain off any liquid. Set aside.

❀ Meanwhile, drain the shiitake mushrooms, reserving the liquid. Squeeze all the liquid from the mushrooms and pat them dry with paper towels. Remove the tough stems and sliver the caps. Set aside.

❀ Preheat an oven to 400°F (200°C). Oil a roasting pan. Place the squash halves, cut sides down, in the pan. Roast until the edges are soft but the centers are firm, about 35 minutes. Remove from the oven, turn cut-sides up, and spoon ½ teaspoon maple syrup into each cavity.

❀ While the squash is roasting, in a large frying pan over medium-low heat, melt the butter with 1 tablespoon olive oil. Add the onion, celery, and carrot and cook, stirring often, until the onion is translucent and the other vegetables are tender-crisp, about 12 minutes. Season with the marjoram, coarse salt, and pepper. Stir in the mushrooms and sauté for 1 minute. Add the Madeira and continue to cook until it is absorbed, about 2 minutes. If the mixture is too dry, add a few more drops olive oil, then stir in the cooked wild rice, mixing well. If desired, sweeten the stuffing with about 1 teaspoon of the maple syrup. Adjust the seasonings.

❀ Spoon the stuffing into the squash halves, dividing it evenly. Drizzle about 1 tablespoon of the reserved mushroom liquid over each half. Return the squash to the oven and continue to roast until the squash is tender when pierced with a fork, about 30 minutes longer. If the stuffing is browning too fast and drying out, reduce the oven temperature to 350°F (180°C) or loosely tent the squash halves with aluminum foil.

❀ Meanwhile, in a small, dry frying pan over high heat, combine the pecans and a pinch of salt. Toast, shaking the pan constantly, until the nuts begin to brown, 3–4 minutes. Transfer to a paper towel.

❀ Transfer the squash halves to warmed individual plates and sprinkle the pecans on top. Serve immediately.

NUTRITIONAL ANALYSIS PER SERVING: Calories 374 (Kilojoules 1,571); Protein 7 g; Carbohydrates 64 g; Total Fat 14 g; Saturated Fat 3 g; Cholesterol 10 mg; Sodium 271 mg; Dietary Fiber 17 g

Smoky and Spicy Chicken Breasts

PREP TIME: 15 MINUTES

COOKING TIME: 40 MINUTES

INGREDIENTS

½ lb (250 g) baked smoked ham, in one piece

8 boneless chicken breast halves, 6–7 oz (185–220 g) each, with skin intact

coarse salt and ground pepper to taste

2 teaspoons ground coriander

3 tablespoons spicy hot red or green jalapeño pepper jelly, or to taste

½ bunch fresh cilantro (fresh coriander)

2 jalapeño chiles, chopped

The delicious advantage to roasting chicken breasts on a bed of ham is that the meat stays moist while picking up the smoky quality of the ham. Add as much jalapeño pepper jelly as you like to produce a spicy glaze that delivers a little fire.

SERVES 8

❊ Preheat an oven to 400°F (200°C).

❊ Cut the smoked ham into narrow julienne strips about ⅛ inch (3 mm) thick. Scatter the ham over the bottom of a baking dish large enough to hold the chicken in a single layer.

❊ Rinse the chicken breast halves and pat dry with paper towels. Season both sides of each piece with salt and pepper, then rub about ¼ teaspoon of the ground coriander on the skin of each piece. Place the chicken pieces, skin sides up, on top of the ham.

❊ Roast, basting with the pan juices after the first 15 minutes, until the skin is crisp, about 35 minutes total.

❊ Meanwhile, in a small saucepan over high heat, warm the jelly until it melts, about 45 seconds.

❊ Remove the chicken from the oven. Brush or spoon about 1 teaspoon of the jelly on top of the crisp skin of each chicken piece and return the chicken to the oven. Continue roasting until the skin is glazed and the juices run clear when the meat is pierced at the thickest point with a fork, about 5 minutes longer.

❊ Serve the chicken directly from the baking dish. Garnish with cilantro and the chopped jalapeños.

NUTRITIONAL ANALYSIS PER SERVING: Calories 306 (Kilojoules 1,285); Protein 43 g; Carbohydrates 5 g; Total Fat 11 g; Saturated Fat 3 g; Cholesterol 119 mg; Sodium 497 mg; Dietary Fiber 0 g

Yam French Fries

PREP TIME: 25 MINUTES

COOKING TIME: 30 MINUTES

INGREDIENTS

about ½ cup (4 fl oz/125 ml)
    vegetable oil

6–8 large yams

about 2 teaspoons ground cumin,
    or to taste

coarse salt and ground pepper
    to taste

COOKING TIP: You can use this
same recipe to oven-roast potatoes.
Leave out the cumin, if you like, or
substitute a dusting of chili powder
or cayenne pepper for spicy fries.

Once your family samples these crisp, sweet yam fries dusted with nutty, aromatic cumin, they will request them often. No matter how many you cook, don't count on leftovers. You can bake the yams at any temperature required for a roast; the cooking time will be longer at lower temperatures.

SERVES 6–8

❊ Preheat an oven to 425°F (220°C).

❊ Line 2 or 3 rimmed baking sheets with aluminum foil. Generously spread the vegetable oil on the pan bottoms, dividing it evenly.

❊ Peel the yams. Using a sharp knife, cut the yams lengthwise into narrow julienne strips about ¼ inch (6 mm) thick. As the sticks are cut, immediately roll them in the oil on the baking sheets to prevent them from turning black. When all the sticks have been coated, spread them out in a single layer.

❊ Sprinkle the yams in each pan with about ½ teaspoon of the cumin and some salt.

❊ Roast until crisp on the outside and tender on the inside, 25–30 minutes. Transfer to 2 or 3 layers of paper towels to drain briefly. Sprinkle with salt, pepper, and 1–1½ teaspoons cumin, or to taste. Transfer to a warmed dish and serve immediately.

NUTRITIONAL ANALYSIS PER SERVING: Calories 324 (Kilojoules 1,361); Protein 3 g; Carbohydrates 55 g; Total Fat 11 g; Saturated Fat 1 g; Cholesterol 0 mg; Sodium 19 mg; Dietary Fiber 8 g

Niçoise Mushrooms

PREP TIME: 15 MINUTES

COOKING TIME: 20 MINUTES

INGREDIENTS

2 tablespoons olive oil

4 salt-cured anchovies, halved and filleted

about 2 tablespoons milk

2 large cloves garlic, chopped

½ teaspoon dried rosemary

½ teaspoon dried thyme

½ teaspoon dried lavender

1½ lb (750 g) small to medium fresh button mushrooms, brushed clean and stems removed

coarse salt and ground pepper to taste

PREP TIP: Salt-cured anchovies are usually found in cans in Italian shops or specialty-food stores. Use what you need, then cover the remaining anchovies with fresh coarse salt and store in the refrigerator.

The woodsy character of the mushrooms is heightened by the lemony floral scent of the herbs and the piquant anchovies. Roast mushrooms are the perfect accompaniment to prepare while roasting meat. To do so, roast them at the temperature suggested for the meat; the cooking time will be shorter at higher temperatures. As a serving alternative, chop the roasted mushrooms together with enough of the cooking liquid to bind them, season to taste, and serve the resulting pâté on toast points.

SERVES 6–8

❀ Preheat an oven to 400°F (200°C). Spread the olive oil on the bottom of a baking dish large enough to hold the mushrooms in a single layer.

❀ Place the anchovies in a single layer in a small shallow bowl. Pour on enough milk nearly to cover them and let stand for 5–10 minutes. Drain off the milk and discard. Pat the anchovies dry with paper towels, removing any tiny bones in the process.

❀ On a cutting board, chop together the anchovies, garlic, rosemary, thyme, and lavender until the mixture is evenly minced but not reduced to a paste.

❀ Place the mushrooms in the prepared baking dish and toss to coat evenly with the oil. Sprinkle the anchovy mixture evenly over the mushrooms. Season with salt and pepper.

❀ Roast the mushrooms until tender, 15–17 minutes depending upon their size. Remove from the oven and transfer to a warmed serving dish. Serve hot.

NUTRITIONAL ANALYSIS PER SERVING: Calories 68 (Kilojoules 286); Protein 3 g; Carbohydrates 5 g; Total Fat 5 g; Saturated Fat 1 g; Cholesterol 2 mg; Sodium 90 mg; Dietary Fiber 1 g

Oven-Baked Brown Rice with Roast Tomatoes

PREP TIME: 10 MINUTES

COOKING TIME: 1 HOUR

INGREDIENTS

8 firm yet ripe plum (Roma) tomatoes, seeded and coarsely chopped

coarse salt and ground pepper to taste

1 teaspoon unsalted butter

2 tablespoons olive oil

1 yellow onion, chopped

2 cups (14 oz/440 g) short-grain brown rice

1 tablespoon chopped fresh thyme, plus sprigs for garnish

4¼ cups (34 fl oz/1 l) chicken broth, heated

MAKE-AHEAD TIP: To prepare this dish in advance, cook as directed, remove from the oven, and immediately place a double thickness of paper towel under the lid to absorb the condensation. Replace the lid, let cool to room temperature, and refrigerate. Bring to room temperature before reheating. Remove the paper towels, re-cover, and reheat in a 325°F (165°C) oven until hot, about 30 minutes. Fluff with a fork and serve.

Roasting in the oven makes this rich, creamy rice dish so easy to prepare that it requires virtually no attention, yet it develops a consistency that recalls a classic risotto. To approximate a risotto even more closely, add a fistful of freshly grated Parmesan cheese and a hefty dollop of butter just before serving.

SERVES 8

❊ Preheat an oven to 400°F (200°C). Line a rimmed baking sheet with aluminum foil. Sprinkle the tomatoes with salt and spread them out on the prepared baking sheet. Roast until the edges of the skins are browned but not burned, 10–12 minutes. Remove from the oven and set aside. Reduce the oven temperature to 375°F (190°C).

❊ Meanwhile, in a dutch oven or a large, heavy heatproof saucepan with a lid over medium heat, melt the butter with the oil. Add the onion and sauté until soft and translucent, about 5 minutes. Add the rice and chopped thyme and season with salt and pepper. Continue to cook, stirring constantly, until the rice is shiny, about 3 minutes.

❊ Stir in the roast tomatoes, then pour in the hot broth. Stir once, cover, and bring to a boil. Transfer to the oven and cook, covered, until all the liquid is absorbed, 40–45 minutes. To test for doneness, tilt the baking dish to one side. If the rice moves, continue cooking until all the liquid is absorbed; if the rice clings to the top edges of the baking dish, it is done.

❊ Remove the rice from the oven and fluff with a fork. Transfer to a warmed serving bowl. Garnish with thyme sprigs and serve immediately.

NUTRITIONAL ANALYSIS PER SERVING: Calories 232 (Kilojoules 974); Protein 5 g; Carbohydrates 43 g; Total Fat 7 g; Saturated Fat 1 g; Cholesterol 1 mg; Sodium 536 mg; Dietary Fiber 4 g

Balsamic Vidalia Blossoms

PREP TIME: 15 MINUTES

COOKING TIME: 35 MINUTES

INGREDIENTS

8 large Vidalia or other sweet onions

coarse salt and ground pepper
  to taste

2 tablespoons balsamic vinegar

about 1½ tablespoons olive oil

⅓ cup (½ oz/15 g) chopped fresh
  flat-leaf (Italian) parsley

Roasting slowly caramelizes the natural sugars in onions, giving them a rich, sweet, mellow flavor that is highlighted by the balsamic vinegar. The onions can be roasted at the same time as the main dish; increase the cooking time when roasting at a lower temperature. The onions are a nice complement to basted meats and fowl, and make a splendid addition to an antipasto platter.

SERVES 8

❉ Preheat an oven to 400°F (200°C). Oil the bottom of a baking dish or pie dish large enough to hold the onions in a single layer.

❉ Working with 1 onion at a time, peel the skin from the top of the onion, trimming off the long hairs but leaving the root end intact. Using a sharp knife and starting at the stem end, cut the onion into eighths or tenths almost through to the root end. Be careful not to cut all the way through. Using your thumbs, pull the onion open slightly to form a blossom shape. Set the onions, root ends down, in the prepared dish; they should be touching but not packed. Season with salt and pepper, then drizzle with the vinegar and olive oil.

❉ Roast until tender when pierced with a fork and the tips are browned, about 35 minutes. Transfer to a warmed platter and garnish with the parsley. Serve immediately.

NUTRITIONAL ANALYSIS PER SERVING: Calories 162 (Kilojoules 680); Protein 6 g; Carbohydrates 32 g; Total Fat 3 g; Saturated Fat 0 g; Cholesterol 0 mg; Sodium 37 mg; Dietary Fiber 6 g

Potato Pancake

PREP TIME: 15 MINUTES

COOKING TIME: 55 MINUTES

INGREDIENTS

3–4 tablespoons olive oil

4 or 5 large baking potatoes

2 teaspoons coarse salt, or to taste

ground pepper to taste

¼ teaspoon Hungarian paprika, or
to taste

½ bunch fresh flat-leaf (Italian)
parsley, stems discarded and
leaves chopped

COOKING TIP: To prepare this with
cheese, omit the salt on the last layer
and scatter about ⅓ cup (1½ oz/45 g)
grated Parmesan cheese or ½ cup
(2 oz/60 g) shredded Swiss or cheddar
cheese evenly over the top. Reduce
the oven temperature to 400°F
(200°C); watch carefully so the top
does not burn.

Totally unpretentious, this crispy pancake, with its soft, tender
interior, will bring accolades from everyone at the dinner table.

SERVES 6

❀ Preheat an oven to 425°F (220°C). Oil a ceramic 11-inch (28-cm)
quiche dish or a glass 10-inch (25-cm) pie dish with 1 teaspoon of the
olive oil.

❀ Shred the potatoes into a bowl, working as quickly as possible to prevent them from turning brown. Transfer the shredded potatoes, a few
handfuls at a time, to the prepared dish. Sprinkle each batch with some
of the coarse salt, a few grindings of pepper, and a few drops of olive oil.
Repeat the layering until the potatoes are level with the rim of the dish.
Drizzle the top with the remaining olive oil, then season with salt, pepper, and the paprika.

❀ Roast until the potatoes are dark brown and crisp on top yet soft
inside when pierced with a fork, 50–55 minutes. If the potatoes begin
to brown too quickly, reduce the oven temperature to 350°F (180°C).

❀ Remove from the oven and let rest for 5–10 minutes, then cut into
wedges. Sprinkle with the parsley and serve immediately.

NUTRITIONAL ANALYSIS PER SERVING: Calories 171 (Kilojoules 718); Protein 3 g;
Carbohydrates 23 g; Total Fat 8 g; Saturated Fat 1 g; Cholesterol 0 mg; Sodium 500 mg;
Dietary Fiber 2 g

Roast Red New Potato Salad

PREP TIME: 20 MINUTES

COOKING TIME: 1 HOUR, PLUS
  1 HOUR FOR CHILLING

INGREDIENTS

3 lb (1.5 kg) red new potatoes

about ⅔ cup (5 oz/155 g) coarse salt

2 tablespoons dry white wine

2 tablespoons extra-virgin olive oil

3 tablespoons sherry wine vinegar

4 shallots, coarsely chopped

3 tablespoons fresh tarragon leaves

¾ cup (6 fl oz/180 ml) olive oil

2 tablespoons Dijon mustard

ground pepper to taste

3 green (spring) onions, chopped

½ bunch fresh flat-leaf (Italian)
  parsley, chopped

PREP TIP: If fresh tarragon is not available, chop 1 tablespoon dried tarragon with 3 tablespoons of the parsley leaves to release the aromatic oils of the dried tarragon.

The secret to great-tasting potato salad is to dress the potatoes while they are hot, so they will absorb the aromatic flavors of the shallots, tarragon, sherry vinegar, and mustard. You can roast these potatoes at any temperature necessary to pair them with meat; the cooking time will be less at higher temperatures. Although this tastes wonderful after marinating overnight in the refrigerator, it is also delicious served as soon as it is made.

SERVES 8

❀ Preheat an oven to 400°F (200°C).

❀ Scrub the potatoes but do not peel. Place in a baking pan large enough to hold them in a single layer and pour the coarse salt generously over them. Roast until tender but firm when pierced, 50–60 minutes depending upon the size of the potatoes.

❀ Remove the potatoes from the oven and, using two pot holders, rub off the excess salt from each one. Place on a cutting board and cut into narrow slices. (If they are still very hot, hold with a pot holder or paper towel as you slice.) Transfer to a bowl. Immediately drizzle the wine, extra-virgin olive oil, and 1 tablespoon of the vinegar over the hot potatoes. Toss gently and set aside.

❀ In a food processor, combine the shallots and tarragon and process to chop finely. Add to the potatoes and toss gently.

❀ In a small bowl, whisk together the olive oil, the remaining 2 tablespoons vinegar, and the mustard. Season with pepper. Pour the dressing over the potatoes, cover with plastic wrap, and refrigerate for at least 1 hour or up to 2 days.

❀ Remove the potato salad from the refrigerator. Add the green onions and parsley and toss gently. Taste and adjust the seasonings. If desired, let stand for about 1 hour before serving. Transfer to a bowl and serve.

NUTRITIONAL ANALYSIS PER SERVING: Calories 361 (Kilojoules 1,516); Protein 4 g; Carbohydrates 32 g; Total Fat 24 g; Saturated Fat 3 g; Cholesterol 0 mg; Sodium *unable to determine;* Dietary Fiber 3 g

Baby Artichokes with Sunflower Seeds

PREP TIME: 20 MINUTES

COOKING TIME: 35 MINUTES

INGREDIENTS

2 tablespoons extra-virgin olive oil,
  or as needed

3 lemons

8 baby artichokes, each 1½–2¼ inches
  (4–5.5 cm) in diameter

2 tablespoons shelled sunflower
  seeds

1 teaspoon snipped fresh chives,
  plus extra for garnish

½ teaspoon dried summer savory

coarse salt and ground pepper
  to taste

Use only the freshest and smallest artichokes for these tempting hors d'oeuvres topped with crunchy sunflower seeds. Serve as a side dish, alone as a starter, or as part of a luncheon salad platter. You can roast the artichokes at any temperature required for another dish, adjusting the cooking time as necessary.

SERVES 8

❋ Preheat an oven to 425°F (220°C). Oil the bottom of a baking dish or pie dish large enough to hold the artichokes in a single layer with the 2 tablespoons olive oil.

❋ Have ready a large bowl of water to which you have added the juice of 1 lemon. Cut the remaining 2 lemons in half. Working with 1 artichoke at a time, cut off the stem even with the base. Break off the tough outer leaves until you reach the paler inner green leaves. Cut off the prickly tops of the leaves, then cut the artichokes in half lengthwise. Immediately rub the exposed parts with the cut side of a lemon half. Drop the artichokes into the lemon water. Repeat until all the artichokes are trimmed.

❋ In a small, dry frying pan over high heat, toast the sunflower seeds, shaking the pan constantly, until they are aromatic, about 3 minutes. Remove from the heat and transfer to a food processor. Pulse once or twice to chop coarsely, then transfer to a small bowl. Add the 1 teaspoon chives, the summer savory, and the salt and pepper. Mix well; set aside.

❋ Drain the artichokes and pat dry. Roll them in the oil in the prepared dish, adding more oil if necessary to coat each artichoke half completely. Arrange the artichokes, cut sides down, in the pan and roast until the leaves are lightly browned and the hearts are still firm in the center, 10–12 minutes. Turn over, sprinkle the sunflower-seed mixture evenly over the top, then spoon some oil from the bottom of the dish over the seed mixture. Continue to roast, basting with oil from the bottom of the dish once or twice, until the edges are browned and crisp and the hearts are fork tender, about 20 minutes longer.

❋ Transfer to a warmed platter and sprinkle with salt. Garnish with chives and serve immediately.

NUTRITIONAL ANALYSIS PER SERVING: Calories 59 (Kilojoules 248); Protein 1 g; Carbohydrates 3 g; Total Fat 5 g; Saturated Fat 1 g; Cholesterol 0 mg; Sodium 16 mg; Dietary Fiber 1 g

Black Plums en Croûte

PREP TIME: 20 MINUTES

COOKING TIME: 45 MINUTES

INGREDIENTS

½ cup (4 oz/125 g) unsalted butter,
at room temperature

1 cup (8 oz/250 g) sugar

1¼ cups (6½ oz/200 g) all-purpose
(plain) flour

½ teaspoon ground cinnamon

½ teaspoon salt

¼ teaspoon baking powder

8 or 9 tart, firm, slightly underripe
black plums, each 2–2¼ inches
(5–5.5 cm) in diameter

½ cup (4 fl oz/125 ml) heavy (double)
cream

½ cup (4 fl oz/125 ml) half-and-half
(half cream)

1 egg

½ teaspoon almond extract (essence)

PREP TIP: The best way to cut a plum
in half is to cut completely around
its circumference, following the natural indent on the fruit. Then, grasp-
ing each half of the plum with the
fingers of each hand, twist the halves
in opposite directions. Dislodge the
pit and discard.

The cinnamon-cookie-like crust makes a perfect platform for the tartness of the plums. A thin layer of almond-scented custard surrounding each piece of fruit mellows the flavor even more. If there are any leftovers, this dessert is a great breakfast for a lucky early riser. For a nice touch, sprinkle the top with brown sugar.

SERVES 6–8

❀ Preheat an oven to 400°F (200°C). In a food processor, combine the butter and sugar and process until fluffy, about 1 minute. Add the flour, cinnamon, salt, and baking powder. Process until the mixture is crumbly. Remove about ¼ cup (2 oz/60 g) of the mixture and set it aside.

❀ Transfer the remaining crumb mixture to a 9-by-13-inch (23-by-33-cm) baking dish or an 11-inch (28-cm) quiche dish. Pat and press the mixture evenly over the bottom and about 1 inch (2.5 cm) up the sides. Quarter the plums lengthwise, discarding their pits. Arrange them in a single layer on top of the crust, exposing part of the pulp and all of the skin and leaving room around each piece. Sprinkle the reserved crumb mixture around the plums. Roast for 20 minutes.

❀ Meanwhile, in a glass measuring pitcher, whisk together the cream, half-and-half, and egg until well mixed. Add the almond extract. Set aside.

❀ After the plums have roasted for 20 minutes, remove from the oven, pour the egg mixture evenly over them, return to the oven, and continue to roast until a knife inserted into the center of the custard comes out clean, about 25 minutes longer. Transfer to a rack and let cool.

❀ To serve, cut into squares or wedges and serve at room temperature.

NUTRITIONAL ANALYSIS PER SERVING: Calories 474 (Kilojoules 1,991); Protein 5 g; Carbohydrates 64 g; Total Fat 23 g; Saturated Fat 14 g; Cholesterol 95 mg; Sodium 208 mg; Dietary Fiber 2 g

Pepper-and-Vanilla–Glazed Pineapple with Yogurt Cheese

PREP TIME: 25 MINUTES,
    PLUS 12 HOURS FOR
    CHILLING

COOKING TIME: 25 MINUTES

INGREDIENTS

1 cup (8 oz/250 g) nonfat plain
    yogurt

1 large ripe pineapple

¼ teaspoon vanilla extract (essence),
    or as needed, plus ¼ teaspoon

½ cup (4 oz/125 g) firmly packed
    light brown sugar

½ teaspoon ground ginger

¼–½ teaspoon ground pepper

1 tablespoon chopped crystallized
    ginger

1 cup (6 oz/185 g) golden or red
    cherries, stems intact, or any
    seasonal berries such as raspberries
    or strawberries

confectioners' (icing) sugar

HEALTHY TIP: For a sugar-free
dessert, glaze the pineapples with
the vanilla-flavored pineapple juices,
omitting the brown sugar glaze.

Freshly ground black pepper is generally considered a seasoning for meats and vegetables, but here the popular spice counterpoints the sweetness of the brown-sugar glaze.

SERVES 6

✸ Line a sieve with dampened cheesecloth (muslin) and place over a bowl. Spoon the yogurt into the sieve, cover, and refrigerate for 12–18 hours. Transfer the resulting yogurt cheese to a storage container, cover, and refrigerate for up to 3 weeks. You should have about ½ cup (4 oz/125 g).

✸ Preheat an oven to 425°F (220°C). Using a long slicing knife, cut down the length of the pineapple to remove the skin. Cut along either side of each row of "eyes" (marked by nature in a diagonal pattern) at a slight angle, to remove them in a shallow wedge. Cut the pineapple in half lengthwise. Cut away the core and place each half, flat side down, on the cutting board. Cut crosswise into slices ½ inch (12 mm) thick.

✸ Pour any accumulated juices from the cutting board into a small bowl and stir in the vanilla extract, using ¼ teaspoon vanilla for every 2 tablespoons pineapple juice.

✸ Arrange the pineapple slices, slightly overlapping, in a fan shape in a shallow baking dish. Drizzle on the flavored pineapple juice. If there are no juices, simply sprinkle the vanilla extract directly onto the slices.

✸ In another small bowl, stir together the brown sugar, ground ginger, and the pepper. Sprinkle the mixture evenly over the pineapple. Roast until the pineapple is glazed on top and tender when pierced with a fork, 20–25 minutes, depending upon the ripeness of the pineapple. Let cool.

✸ Whisk the remaining ¼ teaspoon vanilla extract into the yogurt cheese, then mix in the crystallized ginger. Taste and correct the sweetness.

✸ To serve, arrange 2 or 3 slices glazed pineapple on individual plates. Spoon some of the accumulated cooking juices over the slices, and top with a dollop of the yogurt cheese. Garnish with the cherries or berries and dust with confectioners' sugar, if desired.

NUTRITIONAL ANALYSIS PER SERVING: Calories 192 (Kilojoules 806); Protein 7 g; Carbohydrates 41 g; Total Fat 1 g; Saturated Fat 0 g; Cholesterol 0 mg; Sodium 63 mg; Dietary Fiber 1 g

Roast Bananas with Cinnamon Ice Cream and Chocolate Sauce

PREP TIME: 10 MINUTES

COOKING TIME: 30 MINUTES

INGREDIENTS

FOR THE BANANAS

6 large, firm yet ripe bananas, peeled
  and left whole

about ¼ teaspoon ground cinnamon

about ¼ teaspoon ground nutmeg

1–2 tablespoons granulated sugar,
  or to taste

about 2 tablespoons heavy (double)
  cream

FOR THE CHOCOLATE SAUCE

12 oz (375 g) semisweet (plain)
  chocolate, cut into chunks

2 oz (60 g) unsweetened chocolate,
  cut into chunks

1½–1⅔ cups (12–13 fl oz/375–410 ml)
  heavy (double) cream

1 tablespoon vanilla extract (essence),
  or to taste

1½ qt (1.5 l) cinnamon ice cream
  (see note)

MAKE-AHEAD TIP: The sauce can be
cooled, covered, and refrigerated for
up to 3 weeks; reheat in a small bowl
set over (but not touching) a pan of
barely simmering water.

While the bananas are roasting, the heavy cream and the banana juices meld into a thick sauce. These same bananas, served without the ice cream and chocolate sauce, are an excellent accompaniment to meats, in the Jamaican tradition. If you cannot find cinnamon-flavored ice cream, substitute vanilla or coffee ice cream sprinkled with ground cinnamon.

SERVES 6

✹ Preheat an oven to 375°F (190°C).

✹ Arrange the bananas in a 9-inch (23-cm) pie dish or baking dish. Lightly dust them with the cinnamon, nutmeg, and granulated sugar. Drizzle in enough heavy cream to cover the bottom of the dish.

✹ Roast until the bananas are soft when pierced with a knife but still hold their shape and the reduced cream forms a bubbly sauce, about 30 minutes.

✹ Meanwhile, make the chocolate sauce: In a large heatproof bowl set over (but not touching) simmering water in a saucepan, melt the chocolates together. Pour in the cream in a steady stream, whisking constantly until well incorporated. The chocolate may "seize," that is, become lumpy for a moment or two. Just continue to whisk until the sauce becomes smooth. Stir in the vanilla; taste and adjust the flavoring. Keep hot. You should have about 2½ cups (20 fl oz/625 ml).

✹ When the bananas are ready, arrange them on individual plates, and drizzle their bubbly sauce over them. Serve with a scoop of cinnamon ice cream drizzled with 1 tablespoon of the hot chocolate sauce. Pass the remaining hot chocolate sauce at the table.

NUTRITIONAL ANALYSIS PER SERVING: Calories 959 (Kilojoules 4,028); Protein 11 g; Carbohydrates 106 g; Total Fat 62 g; Saturated Fat 38 g; Cholesterol 151 mg; Sodium 141 mg; Dietary Fiber 4 g

Honey-Pecan Roast Pears

PREP TIME: 15 MINUTES

COOKING TIME: 30 MINUTES

INGREDIENTS

6 large, firm yet ripe pears such as Anjou, Bartlett (Williams'), or Bosc

1 lemon, zest grated and fruit cut in half

about 4 tablespoons (3 oz/90 g) fragrant blossom honey such as clover or wildflower

about 2 tablespoons orange juice

1 cup (4 oz/125 g) pecan halves

1 cup (6 oz/185 g) mixed dry cereals such as a mixture of oat, wheat flake, and toasted granola

¼ cup (2 oz/60 g) firmly packed light brown sugar

1 cup (8 fl oz/250 ml) heavy (double) cream

½ teaspoon vanilla extract (essence), or to taste

For an easy, old-fashioned dessert, serve these crunchy-topped, honey-coated pears with whipped cream. You may use plums or apples in place of the pears.

SERVES 6

❀ Preheat an oven to 375°F (190°C).

❀ Peel the pears, cut in half lengthwise, and core. Immediately squeeze the lemon juice from both halves over the pears. Cut the pears lengthwise into thick slices and arrange in a baking dish or pie dish large enough to hold them in a single layer. Drizzle 1½–2 tablespoons of the honey over the top and add enough orange juice to form a light film on the bottom of the dish. Roast the pears for 10 minutes.

❀ Meanwhile, in a small, dry frying pan over high heat, toast the pecans, shaking the pan constantly, until they are aromatic, 3–4 minutes.

❀ Remove from the heat and reserve several pecan halves for garnish. Transfer the remaining nuts to a food processor and chop coarsely. Add the cereals, lemon zest, and brown sugar and process until evenly chopped and well mixed. Spoon the cereal mixture over the partially roasted pears, forming a "crust." Drizzle with 2–3 more teaspoons of the honey. Continue to roast until the crust is browned on top and the pears are tender when pierced, 15–18 minutes longer.

❀ Meanwhile, in a bowl, whisk the remaining 1 tablespoon honey into the cream. Beat until soft peaks form, then fold in the vanilla.

❀ Remove the pears from the oven. Spoon a dollop of whipped cream on each serving, garnish with the reserved pecan halves, and serve immediately.

NUTRITIONAL ANALYSIS PER SERVING: Calories 585 (Kilojoules 2,457); Protein 7 g; Carbohydrates 80 g; Total Fat 31 g; Saturated Fat 11 g; Cholesterol 54 mg; Sodium 226 mg; Dietary Fiber 8 g

Herb-Glazed Stuffed Figs

PREP TIME: 15 MINUTES,
PLUS 3 HOURS FOR
STEEPING

COOKING TIME: 10 MINUTES

INGREDIENTS

1¼ cups (10 oz/315 g) sugar

1 cup (8 fl oz/250 ml) water

1 tablespoon fresh lemon thyme
leaves, bruised

3–4 tablespoons hulled green
pumpkin seeds

2 pinches of salt

12 firm yet ripe figs

about 6 oz (185 g) mild fresh goat
cheese

grated zest of ½ lemon

grated zest of ½ lime

PREP TIP: If figs are unavailable,
substitute firm yet ripe plums,
halved and pitted. Check to see if
they are done after 4 minutes.

In this simple dessert, the lemon thyme–scented sugar syrup
nearly caramelizes in the bottom of the baking dish, creating a
delectable contrast to the flavors and textures of the juicy figs,
creamy cheese, and crunchy nuts. It's also a great dish to serve
for breakfast. Use the leftover syrup to glaze meat, as a base for
ice cream, or in place of sugar for sweetening fruit.

SERVES 6

❀ In a small saucepan set over high heat, combine the sugar and water
and bring to a boil, stirring to dissolve the sugar. Boil for 2 minutes,
then remove from the heat. Add the lemon thyme leaves, cover, and
let steep for at least 3 hours or for up to 24 hours at room temperature.
Transfer the sugar syrup to a glass jar, cover tightly, and refrigerate.
You should have 1 cup (8 fl oz/250 ml); it will keep for up to 2 weeks.

❀ Preheat an oven to 500°F (260°C).

❀ In a small, dry frying pan over high heat, toast the pumpkin seeds
with a pinch of salt, shaking the pan constantly, until the seeds are
aromatic, lightly browned on the edges, and begin to make a popping
sound, 3–4 minutes. Transfer to paper towels and set aside.

❀ Using a paring knife and starting from the stem end of each fig, cut
the fig about three-fourths of the way through into quarters, leaving the
bottom intact. Place the figs in a single layer in a shallow baking dish;
set aside.

❀ In a bowl, combine the cheese, lemon and lime zests, and the remaining pinch of salt, mixing until well combined. Add about 1 tablespoon of
the sugar syrup to the mixture; taste and adjust the sweetness. Stir in the
toasted seeds. Fill the center of each fig with the cheese mixture, dividing it evenly; each fig will hold 2–3 teaspoons. Drizzle about 1 teaspoon
of the sugar syrup over each fig.

❀ Roast until the cheese melts, 5–7 minutes. Remove from the oven and
place 2 figs on each individual dessert plate. Drizzle the thick syrup from
the bottom of the baking dish over the figs, and serve immediately.

NUTRITIONAL ANALYSIS PER SERVING: Calories 382 (Kilojoules 1,604); Protein 7 g;
Carbohydrates 73 g; Total Fat 9 g; Saturated Fat 5 g; Cholesterol 13 mg; Sodium 156 mg;
Dietary Fiber 4 g

Lavender Glazed Apple Tart

PREP TIME: 40 MINUTES, PLUS
1 HOUR FOR STEEPING AND
1½ HOURS FOR CHILLING

COOKING TIME: 1¼ HOURS

INGREDIENTS

FOR THE GLAZE

½ teaspoon dried lavender, bruised

3 tablespoons vanilla extract
  (essence)

1 tablespoon granulated sugar

2 tablespoons maple syrup

FOR THE PASTRY

3 cups (15 oz/470 g) all-purpose
  (plain) flour

½ teaspoon salt

1 cup (8 oz/250 g) chilled unsalted
  butter, cut into small pieces

1 egg, beaten

6–8 tablespoons (3–4 fl oz/90–125 ml)
  ice water

FOR THE FILLING

4 or 5 large tart green apples such
  as Granny Smith, peeled, halved,
  and cored

1 tablespoon chilled unsalted butter,
  cut into tiny squares

1 tablespoon granulated sugar

FOR THE WHIPPED CREAM

1 tablespoon vanilla glaze, or to taste

1 cup (8 fl oz/250 ml) chilled heavy
  (double) cream, beaten to stiff
  peaks with 1 teaspoon confectioners' (icing) sugar

❀ To make the glaze, in a small saucepan over medium-low heat, combine the lavender, vanilla, and granulated sugar. Heat, stirring, until the mixture is warm. Whisk until the sugar is dissolved, about 1 minute. Remove from the heat and whisk in the maple syrup. Cover and let steep for 1 hour. Strain into a clean jar; you should have about 6 tablespoons (3 fl oz/90 ml). Refrigerate until needed; it will keep indefinitely.

❀ To make the pastry, in a food processor, combine the flour and salt and pulse once or twice to mix. Add the butter and, using on-off pulses, process until the mixture resembles coarse meal. Transfer to a bowl. In a small bowl, beat the egg with 2 tablespoons of the ice water. Make a well in the center of the flour mixture. Add the egg mixture and about 2 more tablespoons ice water to the well. Using a fork, mix lightly, adding more ice water as needed until the mixture holds together. Pat into a ball and wrap in plastic wrap. Refrigerate for at least 1 hour or for up to 4 hours.

❀ On a lightly floured work surface, roll out the pastry into a round about 13 inches (33 cm) in diameter. Transfer to an 11-inch (28-cm) tart pan with a removable bottom, turn under the edges, and prick the bottom in several places with a fork. Press a piece of aluminum foil, shiny side down, onto the crust, and freeze until hard, about 30 minutes.

❀ Preheat an oven to 400°F (200°C). To make the filling, cut off the flower and stem ends of the apples and chop coarsely. Cut the halves lengthwise into slices ¼ inch (6 mm) thick. Remove the foil from the crust and mound the chopped apple in the center. Beginning at the outer edge, arrange the apple slices, overlapping and in concentric circles, until the entire crust is covered. Dot with the butter and sprinkle with the granulated sugar. Bake until the butter melts, about 10 minutes.

❀ Brush the glaze generously over the apple slices. Continue baking, brushing with the glaze two or three more times (reserve about 1½ tablespoons glaze) until the apples are browned and tender, about 1 hour. (If the tart is browning too fast, reduce the temperature to 375°F/190°C.) Transfer to a rack, brush immediately with more glaze, and let cool.

❀ Just before serving, fold the remaining glaze into the whipped cream. Serve the tart with dollops of the cream.

NUTRITIONAL ANALYSIS PER SERVING: Calories 544 (Kilojoules 2,285); Protein 7 g; Carbohydrates 55 g; Total Fat 33 g; Saturated Fat 20 g; Cholesterol 118 mg; Sodium 150 mg; Dietary Fiber 3 g

GLOSSARY

CHILES

A wide variety of chiles can contribute a pleasant glow of heat, along with a subtle hint of mellow sweetness, to roast dishes. In addition, roasting chiles deepens their flavor while transforming the texture of fresh chiles from crisp to tender. Well-stocked food stores and Hispanic and farmers' markets offer the best selection of chiles, including those used in this book: large, slender green **Anaheims**, a mild to slightly hot variety also referred to as the long green or California chile; spicy, sweet, and fruity **ancho chiles** (the dried form of the red poblano chile), distinguished by their brick-red, wrinkled skin and wide stem ends; fiery-hot fresh or dried red **árbol chiles**, slender, tapered, and 2–3 inches (5–7.5 cm) long; mildly spicy, dark green or sometimes ripened red **poblano chiles**, which resemble tapered, triangular bells measuring up to 5 inches (13 cm) in length and 3 inches (7.5 cm) in width; and familiar, fiery green **jalapeños**, thick-fleshed, tapered in shape and measuring 2–3 inches (5–7.5 cm) long and up to 1½ inches (4 cm) at their stem ends. The latter are also smoke-dried to make **chipotle chiles**, most commonly sold canned in a thick vinegar-based adobo sauce.

When you work with any chiles, always bear in mind that their heat comes from volatile oils that can also cause a painful burning sensation in your eyes, cuts on your hands, or other sensitive areas. After handling the peppers, wash your hands thoroughly with warm, soapy water. Alternatively, wear kitchen gloves.

CORN

With its sweet and mellow flavor, fresh corn makes a wonderful companion to roast dishes during its season, which stretches from summer into autumn. For the best quality, buy recently harvested corn; farmers' markets and roadside stands are likely to offer the freshest selection. Pull back the green husks and fine silks, which themselves should look fresh and pale in color, to check that the kernels beneath are plump and smooth.

To cut the kernels from an ear of corn, first strip away the husks and silk. Holding the ear by its pointed end, steady the stalk end on a cutting board. With a sharp, sturdy knife, cut down and away from you along the ear to strip off several rows of kernels at one time. Turn the ear with each cut to strip the entire cob.

GARLIC

Prized for its pungent and highly aromatic taste, garlic makes a flavorful contribution to many roast dishes and accompaniments. When roasted, its flavor mellows to a rich,

EQUIPMENT

BULB BASTER
Consisting of a long, tapered tube with a rubber bulb at one end, this simple kitchen device is used to suction up juices from the bottom of a roasting pan by squeezing the bulb, then slowly releasing it. To baste with the captured juices, simply squeeze the bulb again and release it, and the juices will flow from the tip. Release them over the surface of a roast to promote browning while maintaining moistness. The tubes of bulb basters may be made of nylon or glass, but the most durable and heat-resistant types are made of stainless steel or aluminum.

CARVING BOARD
Hardwood carving boards both beautifully display whole roasts of meat or poultry at the table and serve a practical purpose. Ridges cut into the surface help to keep the roast from slipping while it is being carved. The ridges also channel the juices that flow from the roast into the groove around the board's perimeter, where they can be retrieved for moistening servings.

CARVING SET
These basic serving tools make carving any main-course roast of meat or poultry easier and more efficient. The sturdy, two-pronged fork steadies the roast and assists the knife in lifting and removing pieces or slices to a serving platter or individual plates. The long blade of the knife has the flexibility to maneuver between poultry joints or meat bones and a keen edge to slice through meats or tendons with equal ease. Select a carving set with high-quality stainless-steel blades that are securely attached to sturdy handles that feel comfortable and secure in your hands.

almost sweet character with none of raw garlic's harshness. For the best flavor, buy whole heads of dry garlic, separating individual cloves from the head as you need them. Do not buy more than you will use in 1–2 weeks.

To peel a clove of garlic, place it on a work surface and press down firmly on it with the side of a knife blade, the bottom of a saucepan, or some other heavy object, loosening the papery skin, which will then slip off easily.

LEEKS

Available from autumn through early spring, these long, cylindrical members of the onion family taste sweet and mild when cooked. The white parts are more tender and finer in flavor and are often used alone. The tougher greens, however, may be included in long-cooked dishes. Grown in sandy soil, leeks should be washed thoroughly under cold running water to remove any grit lodged among their multi-layered leaves.

MUSTARD, DIJON

Dijon mustard, traditionally made in the French city of Dijon from dark brown mustard seeds (unless otherwise marked *blanc*) and white wine or wine vinegar, has a distinctive pale color and moderately hot, sharp flavor. Authentic Dijon mustards are made from finely ground seeds for a smooth, creamy consistency. However, some types labeled "Dijon" are made with whole or partially crushed seeds for a more grainy texture.

NUTMEG

The hard pit of the fruit of the nutmeg tree, this popular sweet spice adds a subtle flavor to both sweet and savory roast dishes and accompaniments. Its taste goes particularly well with roasted fruits. Nutmeg may be bought already ground, but the freshest, fullest flavor comes from whole nutmeg that you grate yourself with a small nutmeg grater designed specifically for that purpose. Store nutmeg in an airtight container in a cool, dark place.

OLIVE OIL

The ripened fruit of the olive tree is pressed and filtered to produce an aromatic, flavorful oil that is used for both cooking and seasoning foods. Although long favored in Mediterranean kitchens, it is now enjoyed throughout the

DUTCH OVEN
This large, deep, heavy ovenproof dish with a tight-fitting lid holds smaller roasts in the oven, creating, in effect, a miniature oven in which they can cook with little loss of moisture. Sometimes referred to as covered casseroles, the most effective dutch ovens are made of cast iron coated with an enamel or porcelain finish.

ROASTING PAN
A heavy, durable metal roasting pan should be large and sturdy enough to hold a roast while allowing ample room for heat to circulate and for basting. Select a sturdy, V-shaped metal roasting rack made of thick stainless-steel rods to hold a roast inside the pan. Because the rack raises the roast off the pan bottom, air circulates for more even cooking and it allows easier access to pan juices for basting. The raised handles facilitate removing the roast from the pan.

THERMOMETER, INSTANT-READ
Inserted into the thickest part of the thigh on roast poultry or into the center of roast meat at the earliest moment at which it might be done cooking, this thermometer quickly and precisely registers the internal temperature for the most reliable test of doneness. If further roasting is required, the thermometer is removed until the next test. For an accurate reading, always take care not to touch bone when inserting the thermometer.

HERBS

Whether used in marinades, as seasonings, or as a garnish to finished dishes, fresh and dried herbs add bright green color and lively flavor to roasts and their accompaniments. To store fresh herbs, refrigerate them, either with their stem ends in a glass of water or wrapped in damp paper towels inside a plastic bag. Buy dried herbs in quantities no greater than you will use in a few months, storing them airtight and away from light and heat.

BASIL

Spicy-sweet, tender-leaved basil, which also comes in such scented varieties as lemon basil and cinnamon basil, goes especially well with chicken, duck, and turkey and in dishes that also feature tomatoes.

BAY LEAF

The dried whole leaves of the bay laurel tree have a pungent, spicy flavor that imparts an aromatic accent to simmered dishes and marinades. Seek out the Turkish variety, which has a milder, sweeter flavor than the California variety. Bay leaves are generally removed from dishes before serving.

CHIVE

This mild herb has a flavor reminiscent of the onion, to which it is related. It is usually added to a dish near the end of cooking, to preserve its distinctive character.

HERBES DE PROVENCE

A typical seasoning of the Provence region of south-central France, this blend of dried herbs is sold commercially, with the elements of the mix varying with the packager. If you wish to make your own, here is a common blend: in a bowl, mix together 3 parts each dried thyme and basil; 2 parts each dried marjoram, crumbled rosemary, and dried lavender or chamomile blossoms; and 1 part each ground dried sage and chopped fennel seeds. Transfer to a glass jar, cover tightly, and store in a cool, dark place.

LAVENDER

The leaves, stems, and, to a lesser extent, the blossoms of this flowering plant have a sweet, highly aromatic flavor that goes well with poultry or lamb. Lavender can be found in the pantries of Provence, as the plant thrives there and is commonly used in the making of soaps, perfumes, and similar products. When buying lavender for cooking purposes, be certain it comes from flowers that were grown free of pesticides.

OREGANO

Also known as wild marjoram, this highly aromatic and spicy herb, a staple of Italian and Greek cooking, is used fresh or dried in all kinds of savory dishes, from roast poultry to tomato sauce.

PARSLEY, FLAT-LEAF

Also known as Italian parsley, this variety of the widely popular fresh herb, native to southern Europe, has a more pronounced flavor than the common curly type, making it preferable as a seasoning.

ROSEMARY

Used either fresh or dried, this Mediterranean herb has a strong, aromatic flavor well suited to meats, poultry, seafood, and vegetables alike. It is particularly popular as a seasoning for roast chicken and lamb.

SUMMER SAVORY

This aromatic green herb, whose flavor bears a slight similarity to rosemary and thyme, goes well with the tastes of vegetables, seafood, and poultry. Both its fresh and dried forms may be used, with dried summer savory widely available in food stores. The closely related winter savory has a sharper flavor.

TARRAGON

Used both fresh and dried, this herb has a distinctively sweet flavor and fragrance reminiscent of anise. Tarragon is a classic seasoning for roast chicken, but also complements lamb and veal.

THYME

A brightly flavored ancient herb of the eastern Mediterranean, thyme may be used fresh or dried. The variety known as lemon thyme has a distinctively citrusy taste that makes it a popular seasoning for seafood. Thyme is also a popular addition to roast poultry dishes.

world. **Extra-virgin olive oil** is the highest grade of oil extracted on the first pressing without use of heat or chemicals. It has a distinctively fruity flavor and color, ranging from pale yellow to dark green, that varies depending upon the particular olives from which it was pressed, just as wines vary depending upon their grapes. It is used primarily to contribute character to dressings or marinades or as a condiment. Products labeled **"pure olive oil"** have undergone further filtering to eliminate much of their character; being less aromatic and flavorful, they are better suited to general cooking purposes.

ONIONS

Onions of all kinds add pungent flavor to roast dishes and their accompaniments. The dry, prolonged heat of roasting helps develop and caramelize an onion's natural sugars, resulting in rich, mellow, and sweet flavors to offset the vegetable's natural pungency.

GREEN ONIONS

Also called spring onions or scallions, these long, slender onions are harvested immature, leaves and all, before their bulbs have had a chance to form. Both their green and white parts are appreciated for their mild but still pronounced onion flavor. Select dry, firm, crisp specimens with undamaged tops.

VIDALIA ONIONS

Resembling large, slightly flattened yellow onions with their brownish skins and white flesh, these onions, grown in and around Vidalia, Georgia, are prized for their distinctively mild, sweet flavor. Other sweet onion varieties may be substituted, including Maui onions (from Hawaii), Walla Wallas (from

Washington State), and some Texas-grown onions typified by the variety known as the 1015 Supersweet.

YELLOW ONIONS

The most commonly available onion, these have white flesh and a strong flavor. They are easily recognized by their dry, yellowish brown skins.

SAFFRON

Perhaps the rarest of spices, saffron, the dried stigmas of a species of crocus, imparts an intensely aromatic flavor and bright golden orange color to classic Mediterranean and Indian dishes. It is sold either as "threads"—the dried stigmas—or crushed in powdered form; the former maintain their flavor longer than the latter.

SALT, COARSE

Coarse-grained, purified rock salt, sold in the seasonings section of food stores, is frequently used in marinades and seasonings. Rubbed on or used as a bed for roasts, it both seasons the food and assists in the formation of a crusty exterior. Coarse salt is also known and sold as kosher salt because it meets the requirements for the preparation of meat in accordance with Jewish dietary laws. More

intensely flavored sea salt, made by evaporating sea water, is an acceptable substitute in recipes calling for coarse salt.

SHALLOTS

These brown-skinned, purple-tinged cousins of onions and garlic, midway in size and shape between the two, are also thought by some to have a flavor resembling a cross between those vegetables.

WATERCRESS

Part of the mustard family, these crisp sprigs of rounded, dark green leaves contribute a refreshingly spicy flavor to salads or add a breezy air as a garnish to a range of savory dishes, including roasts. Watercress grows wild in freshwater streams in its native Europe and elsewhere, but it also thrives in commercial cultivation. It will have the sweetest, least bitter flavor when picked during the cooler months of spring or autumn.

ZEST

The outermost, brightly colored layer of a citrus fruit's rind, rich in essential oils that literally add zest to savory and sweet dishes alike.

Citrus zest may be removed in several ways: in small particles with a fine grater; in thin strips with a swivel-bladed vegetable peeler or a special citrus "stripper"; or in fine shreds with the small, sharp-edged holes of a citrus zester. In every case, care should be taken not to remove any of the thick layer of bitter white pith beneath the zest.

INDEX

ACKNOWLEDGMENTS

The publishers would like to thank the following people and associations for their generous support and assistance in
producing this book: Ken DellaPenta, Jennifer Hanson, Hill Nutrition Associates, Sharilyn Hovind, Lisa Lee, and Cecily Upton.

The following kindly lent props for photography: Fillamento, Williams-Sonoma, and Pottery Barn, San Francisco, CA. The photographer would like to thank
Lisa and Doug Atwood for generously sharing their home with us for our location setting. We would also like to thank Chromeworks and ProCamera, San Francisco, CA,
and FUJI Film for their generous support of this project. Special acknowledgment goes to Daniel Yearwood for the beautiful backgrounds and surface treatments.